A STRONG FUTURE

for Public Library Use and Employment

ALA RESEARCH SERIES

Libraries Connect Communities 3: Public Library Funding and Technology Access Study, American Library Association, University of Maryland, and Florida State University

A Good Match: Library Career Opportunities for Graduates of Liberal Arts Colleges, Rebecca A. Watson-Boone

A STRONG FUTURE
for Public Library Use and Employment

José-Marie Griffiths

AND

Donald W. King

AMERICAN LIBRARY ASSOCIATION

Chicago   2011

Donald W. King is currently Honorary University Professor at Bryant University in Rhode Island and an adjunct professor at the University of Tennessee School of Information Sciences. King, a statistician, cofounded Westat, Inc., a statistical consulting and survey research company, in 1961 and served as president of three research companies—King Research, Home Testing Institute, and Westat Surveys—until the mid-1990s. After retiring, he continued research on a pro bono basis with Drs. José-Marie Griffiths and Carol Tenopir. King's fifty years in research have emphasized economic cost modeling and surveys dealing with libraries and scholarly publishing, as well as marketing research and political polling. His numerous publications include 17 books (4 award-winning) and more than 150 other publications.

King's work been recognized by the Chemical Heritage Foundation (Pioneer in Science Information), the American Statistical Association (Fellow), and the American Society for Information Science and Technology (Research Award and Award of Merit), and has received many other awards and honors.

He received a BS and MS in statistics from the University of Wyoming (1959, 1960).

José-Marie Griffiths is Vice President for Academic Affairs and University Professor at Bryant University in Rhode Island. Her research spans more than 30 years in information science and technology. She has performed groundbreaking work in a wide range of areas. This research and leadership is reflected in several books and more than 100 other publications.

Griffiths's accomplishments have been recognized by several prestigious appointments and awards, including three presidential appointments and service on many blue-ribbon panels and committees. She was elected a fellow of the American Association for the Advancement of Science and received the Award of Merit and the Research Award from the American Society for Information Science and Technology and was also named one of the Top 25 Women on the Web in 1999.

Griffiths completed her undergraduate degree in Physics with honors and a PhD in Information Science from University College London.

Printed in the United States of America

15 14 13 12 11   5 4 3 2 1

Library of Congress Cataloging-in-Publication Data
Griffiths, José-Marie
    A strong future for public library use and employment / José-Marie Griffiths and
  Donald W. King.
       p. cm.—(ALA research series)
    Includes bibliographical references and index.
    ISBN 978-0-8389-3588-0 (alk. paper)
    1. Public libraries—United States—Use studies. 2. Public libraries—United States—
  Statistics. 3. Public librarians—Employment—United States—Statistics. 4. Public
  librarians—Supply and demand—United States. 5. Library surveys—United States.
  I. King, Donald Ward, 1932- II. Title.
    Z678.88.G75 2011
    025.5'874—dc22   2011011677

ISBNs: 978-0-8389-3588-0 (paper); 978-0-8389-9307-1 (PDF). For more information on digital formats, visit the ALA store at alastore.ala.org and select eEditions.

Cover design by Kirsten Krutsch. Text design in Melior and Meta by Dianne M. Rooney.

⊚ This paper meets the requirements of ANSI/NISO Z39.48–1992 (Permanence of Paper).

Dedicated to our children,
Lisa, Kelly, Sara, Mary,
Erin, and Rhiannon,
and
our fourteen
grandchildren

ALA Editions purchases fund advocacy,
awareness, and accreditation programs
for library professionals worldwide.

Contents

WEB Additional material available at www.alaeditions.org/webextras/.

Figures

Tables

Acknowledgments

This book presents excerpts from four studies conducted from 2004 to 2008. The relevant study reports include

Interconnections: The IMLS National Study on the Use of Libraries, Museums, and the Internet

- Public Library Survey Results, March 2008
- General Information Report, January 2008

A National Study of the Future of Public Librarians in the Workforce, June 2009

These and other relevant reports funded by IMLS are available at

www.bryant.edu/libraryworkforce/

www.bryant.edu/interconnectionsreport/

The statewide studies are

Taxpayer Return on Investment in Florida Public Libraries, September 2004

Taxpayer Return-on-Investment (ROI) in Pennsylvania Public Libraries, September 2006

In addition to the authors of this book and those of the reports above, survey staff include: Scott Beach, Chris Briem, Robert Keene, and Janet Schlarb (University of Pittsburgh, University Center for Social and Urban Research); analysts Christinger Tomer and Matt Herbison (University of Pittsburgh, School of Information Sciences); Rabikar Chatterjee (Katz School of Business); Thomas Lynch and Julie Harrington (Florida State University), Sara Aerni, Leo Cao, Songphan Choemprayong and Kathleen J. McClatchey (University of North Carolina at Chapel Hill, School of Information and Library Science) and Joel Popkin (Popkin and Associates).

We particularly thank Denise Davis, editor, who made many helpful suggestions and led us to highly relevant references. We also thank the study sponsors and their staff: the Institute of Museum and Library Services, the Florida Division of Library and Information Services, and the Commonwealth of Pennsylvania, Office of Commonwealth Libraries. The workforce project team included Syracuse University (David Lances), the Association of Research Libraries (Martha Kyrilladou), and the Special Libraries Association (John Latham).

We also appreciate the 5,251 adults who answered household telephone interviews; the 4,119 adults who participated in the surveys conducted in libraries; the 3,892 library staff who participated in the public library staff survey; the 3,339 public libraries that responded to surveys and the 295 other organizations that responded to statewide surveys.

Thank you all,

José-Marie Griffiths

Donald W. King

EXECUTIVE SUMMARY

It may seem like a strange time (2011) to publish a book on *A Strong Future for Public Library Use and Employment.* However, prior to the current recession (2008 and beyond) there had been abundant evidence showing strong positive trends in public library growth, visits, services, operations, and employment with little downside. Furthermore, the use and value of public library services are clearly established, as is a substantial taxpayer return on investment in public libraries. Because of concerns related to the current recession, evidence is presented that relates to public library and employment experiences observed over the past three recessions and as much as possible concerning the current one, with all four recessions occurring around the turns of the past four decades (1980 to 2010). The following evidence is consistent across all four recessions:

- revenue sources declined, requiring adjustments such as reduced expenditures, reduced hours of operation, closing of branches and bookmobiles, and other steps taken to deal with fewer resources;
- use of many services increased substantially and remained at a higher level following the last two recessions; and
- public libraries adjusted to provide services that are particularly needed during recessions, thereby increasing their value to the communities they serve.

Because public libraries play an increasingly important role in their communities, it is critical that this message be communicated to funders and users.

Based on past experience, one would expect public libraries to emerge from the current recession in a stronger position. However, this recession is unlike the previous recessions in that federal, state, and local funders have accumulated substantial deficits that may require unusual cuts and extend the length of the recession. Nevertheless, public libraries must continue to provide their valued services and contribute to their communities.

BACKGROUND

The information environment has changed dramatically in recent decades, particularly due to availability of the public Internet and the World Wide Web. These foundational technological developments created an environment in which almost anyone can "publish" or function as an information provider and both provide and have virtually instantaneous access to massive volumes of information. Libraries have long been sources of recreation, learning, and information for personal, family, educational, and workplace purposes. However, the Internet, Web, and other technologies have become an increasingly used source of information that some believe will replace their physical counterparts. On the other hand, some have speculated that the Internet and related technologies will actually facilitate and increase public library use. This book provides solid evidence that addresses this issue and answers questions concerning the consequences for users' needs and service provision.

The future of librarians has also been the subject of a great deal of speculation due to the tremendous technological changes. More recently, concerns have been expressed about the impending loss of "aging/graying" workers due to death, disability, or retirement. There are serious questions about what the future public library workforce will require, what types of jobs will be necessary, what competencies (i.e., knowledge, skills, and abilities) will be necessary, and whether the supply of qualified librarians will be sufficient to meet the expected demand. This book supplies evidence to answer these questions.

The nation is currently in a severe recession that has librarians and the public they serve wondering how employment and service provision will be affected. To help address this important concern, data are obtained from the past three recessions to determine their impact on funding, employment, and services. Additional evidence examines the impact, thus far, of the current recession on public libraries.

The Institute of Museum and Library Services (IMLS) commissioned two studies under the leadership of the authors of this book. The first study was awarded to the University of Pittsburgh, School of Information Sciences, Sara Fine Institute for Interpersonal Behavior and Technology. It involved national household telephone interviews of adults to establish who information users are, their needs, sources of information used (e.g., publications, people, the Internet, etc.), which providers of the sources are used (e.g., bookstores, libraries, museums, families, workplace, etc.), why information sources and providers are chosen, and what value and outcomes result from the use of the information. The focus was on users of online public library and museum information and the Internet. This study resulted in 5,251 completed interviews. Four principal reports were produced: Public Library Report, Museum Report, Internet Report, and General Information Report.[1] Information and data from the Public Library and General Information reports are extensively used for this book.

The second IMLS study examined the future of librarians in the workforce, including public, academic, special, and school librarians, with reports covering each of the four types of libraries and a combined report.[2] The public library component of this project consisted of five library surveys conducted in 2007, each of which included a common set of questions. The five surveys had a second part addressing in-depth operational issues, services, functions, competencies, and a Staff Survey. The web-based Library Survey had 3,127 total responses, and each of the five parts had approximately one-fifth that number. One survey (692 responses) asked the public libraries to forward a Staff Survey to their staff, resulting in 3,892 individual responses, of which 1,020 were librarians holding a graduate degree from a library and information studies/science (LIS) program accredited by the American Library Association (referred to hereafter as *MLS librarians*). Results from all components of the Library Survey and the Staff Survey are discussed in this book.

Some information and data have come from an annual series of National Center for Educational Statistics (NCES) reports on public libraries from 1990 to 2005. The same series is now provided by the IMLS, with the most recent covering 2007. Also, a study on the supply of and demand for librarians sponsored by the NCES in 1982 provides a good historical perspective. Finally, several studies sponsored by the American Library Association (ALA) confirm and add to the other studies and yield some evidence of the impact of the current recession.

This book is organized into eight chapters in addition to this "Executive Summary." Chapters 2 through 5 focus on public library trends and issues, while chapters 6 through 8 deal with MLS librarian and staff trends. Chapter 9 examines the impact of the previous three recessions on public libraries and gives some indication of the effects of the current recession to date.

WHY PUBLIC LIBRARIES ARE ESSENTIAL

The extensive value of public libraries is well established. People tend to think of public libraries as a place to satisfy the recreational or entertainment needs of patrons through books and other materials and the provision of special programs. Public libraries were visited 1.471 billion times in 2007 by adults (18 and over). However, only 28.9 percent of visits (or 425 million visits) were for recreation or entertainment by checking out materials, reading in the library, listening to music or other recordings, watching a movie, participating in another program, or attending a lecture or other program. Visitors say they benefited in many ways from these recreation or entertainment-related activities, such as encouraging further reading, viewing, or listening; helping them learn something new; inspiring them; broadening their perspective on life; and so on.

In January 2010, 65 percent of adult Americans (about 152.5 million) had used their library in the past year, and some had used it as many as 25 times or more. About 77 percent of households reported using the local library to borrow materials, 40 percent to use reference materials, 67 percent to consult the librarian, 39 percent to read newspapers or magazines, and 24 percent to hear a speaker, see a movie, or attend a special program.

On the other hand, 35.3 percent or 519 million visits (in 2006) and 41 percent (in 2010) of public library visits were made by adults (18 and over) for educational purposes as students researching a topic, working on an assignment, or using the library as a place to study (12 million visits). Teachers frequently use public libraries for continued learning, to keep up with the literature, or prepare for a class or a special lecture (20 million visits). Other adults use the library for continued learning or to perform personal research (26 million visits). In addition, 126 million visits involve small children aged 5 and under to read or check out books, and 459 million visits were made by students (6 to 17) to study or complete classroom assignments.[3] Finally, school and academic libraries are served by public libraries through interlibrary lending and reference advice.

A total of 342 million visits by adults (23.2% of their visits) are made to address personal or family information needs such as looking for health-related information; finance or legal information; information about a hobby or work around the home; to buy something; to help with travel plans; and, during the current recession, to provide substantial support for job hunting or obtaining information from government agencies or determining the services they offer.

Twelve percent or 185 million visits of public libraries by adults are work-related in support of professionals such as lawyers or accountants and small businesses to help with problems in research, administration, finance, marketing and sales, etc. Public libraries also provide substantial services to special libraries in businesses, hospitals, government, and so on.

Public library visitors accounted for a total of about 5 billion uses of library services in 2006. Visitors would not use library services so extensively if they did not gain value from their use. In fact, prior to the current recession, visitors were willing to pay substantially in their time and cost to visit public library services. For example, they averaged spending about 62 minutes per visit in the library and traveling to and from the library, or $18.30 in their time (2008 dollars), and an additional amount of $0.78 driving, parking, and other transportation, per library visit.

If the public libraries did not exist, visitors say they would seek alternative sources of information or services for about 85 percent of their visits. Averaged across all visits, the visitors would have to spend an additional 43 minutes to use the alternative source and $28.20 in other costs for travel, purchasing or renting materials, and so on.

Public libraries also serve other libraries through interlibrary loan, reference, access to licensed databases, etc. Other libraries were asked how much these services saved them in staff time and cost. By using these services, school libraries annually save about $940 per library, academic libraries $5,070, and special libraries $1,050 (all in 2008 dollars).

Clearly, the value of public libraries increases with additional visits. This is found to be true during recessions, when in-person visits increased 40 percent in 2009 from 2006 and visits by computer (remote online) increased by 107 percent during that time and, as mentioned above, the services were adapted to be recession-relevant to users.

Several studies prior to the current recession have examined the return on taxpayer investment in public libraries. These studies have used several alternative approaches to measuring the return where the investment is taxpayer funding from local, state, and federal governments. The returns obtained in various ways range from about 3 to 1 up to 5 to 1. However, during the current recession, because funding is down but visits are up and probably returns are increasing, the return on investment may be unusually high and not tenable over the long term.

LIBRARY VISITS AND SERVICE TRENDS

This section examines the numbers of public library visits and service uses with five-year trends from fiscal year 2002 to fiscal year 2007 based on national reports from the NCES in 2002 and the same type of data provided by the IMLS in 2007. Similar trends are also obtained from a 2007 survey of public libraries where observations were made for 2007 and trends compared to five years earlier. A 2006 Telephone Survey was conducted with adults (18 and over) to estimate the extent of use of public libraries and some recent trends in their use. Finally, the ALA provides useful recent data and information.

While the population served by public libraries had increased by 5.3 percent in 2007 from 2002, the number of libraries increased by only 0.8 percent. During the last two recessions over four years (early 1990s and 2000s) the number of central libraries remained the same in the first recession and increased 1.5 percent in the second.

Generally, the number of visits per capita and the use of library services increased in 2007 from 2002, suggesting that library use had a strong gain. For example, in-person visits per capita increased 8.9 percent, circulation increased 8.8 percent (reflecting visits), and interlibrary borrowing and lending more than doubled in that time. On the other hand, reference transactions actually decreased by 9.1 percent. During the past two recessions the number of in-person visits per capita rose substantially: 32.2 percent in the first one (early 1990s) and 9.3 percent in the early 2000s. These gains are over four years compared with 8.9 percent over the five-year period from 2002 to 2007. In fact, if one considers the additional remote online visits that were made during the second recession, the total visits rose substantially during these recessions. In 2006 there were 223 million adults aged 18 and over who averaged 3.4 in-person visits per adult and 2.6 remote online visits, or a total of 6 visits per adult. This evidence from the 2006 Telephone Survey (as compared to the 8.9 percent from the NCES/IMLS data above) suggests that the increase of 8.8 percent in in-person visits per capita would be substantially higher if remote online visits at that time were included. In-person visits per child under age 18 are estimated to be about 7 visits per child.

There is abundant evidence from the 2006 Telephone Survey that remote visits do not replace in-person visits but rather increase them. Only 4 percent of adults who visited by either means did so by remote visit only. Average in-person visits per visitor are 2.2 times for those who visited remotely 1 to 5 times annually, and increase steadily to 7.3 in-person visits per visitor for those who visited remotely more than 25 times. These findings were largely reaffirmed in the 2010 ALA Household Survey.

Circulation also increased substantially during the last two recessions: 10.3 percent per capita in the early 1990s recession and 10.9 percent in the early 2000s, both over four years. This is compared with a five-year increase of 8.8 percent from 2002 to 2007. The larger increase during recessions may be attributable to users borrowing from public libraries rather than purchasing books and other materials.

Over the years, there has been a general decline in public library reference transactions. For example, from 2002 to 2007 the number of reference transactions per capita decreased about 9 percent. During the early 1990s recession, per-capita transactions increased by 19.6 percent, but during the later (2000s) recession they remained the same at 1.1 transactions per capita each year. It may be that access to

Internet search engines and databases through increased use of in-library workstations (public-use Internet terminals) and from remote access may have displaced
traditional library reference services. For example, 70 percent of remote online visits
involved use of a search engine (e.g., Google or Yahoo), as did 45 percent of in-
person online visits.

The 2006 Telephone Survey showed that adults used the catalog during 35 percent of their in-library visits. The 2007 Library Survey indicated that 91 percent
of libraries provide access to an online catalog in the library and 81 percent from
remote online, and both showed a substantial increase in use compared to five years
previously. Users used reference materials in the library on 36 percent of their visits
and 96 percent of libraries provide them, but use is down some. Similarly, users
asked a librarian for help finding information in the library or on the Internet during
42 percent of their visits and 99 percent of libraries provide the service, but use is
up only slightly. About 40 percent of users used a library workstation and 96 percent
of libraries provide access to them, and 88 percent of libraries say more use is being
made of them. Other services provided include foreign-language assistance (33%
of libraries provide this, with use generally up) and foreign-language materials provided by 75 percent of libraries, with use up; instruction or training in technology,
e-publications, or general bibliographic databases is provided by about half of the
libraries, and use is up. About half the libraries provide technology to support the
visual and hearing-impaired (46% of libraries), materials for the visually impaired
(80%), or materials for the hearing-impaired (43%), with all showing some increase
in use. Public libraries are becoming more technologically competent in providing
wireless networks (65% of libraries), electronic collections (about 50%), and web
portals to resources (75%), all with increasing use.

The 2006 Telephone Survey also revealed that most in-person and remote visitors used public libraries because they are convenient or easy to use (82% and 94%
of visitors, respectively), visits did not cost much in time or money (70% by both
types of visitors), the visits provided the best source of information (76% and 64%),
and the information provided could be trusted (66% and 75%). Evidence shows that
trust in public libraries is established through more use, since many more frequent
users cite trust as a reason for visiting public libraries than infrequent users. These
findings were similarly confirmed in the 2010 ALA Household Survey.

Evidence based on 2002 to 2007 statistics shows strong use of public libraries,
and data during the past two recessions show an even greater use. An important
phenomenon is that the jumps in increased public library visits and service use during recessions remain high following them, suggesting that the experience of using
public libraries more per user or by more users has an influence on subsequent use
patterns. However, the current recession could last well beyond four years, which
might change the pattern.

TREND IN NUMBER OF PUBLIC MLS LIBRARIANS

The IMLS-commissioned workforce study focused on MLS librarians who have a
graduate MLS degree from an LIS program accredited by the American Library Association. These librarians have increased in number (full-time equivalents—FTEs)

nearly every year from the early 1980s to 2007. They increased in number from 30,428 in 2002 to 32,173 in 2007 (i.e., a 5.7% increase). The 2007 Staff Survey reported MLS librarians by head count so that both full-time and part-time staff would be identified, resulting in an increase from 2002 to 2007 of 33,074 to 36,169 (a 9.4% increase), suggesting an increase in part-time librarians as well. Not all public libraries employed MLS librarians. In fact, only 63 percent did in 2007, up from 61 percent in 2002.

The 2007 Staff Survey identified five categories of library staff: MLS librarians (19.9% of staff in 2007), other professionals working in a librarian capacity (5.3%) or in another capacity (3.5%), paraprofessionals (31%), and nonprofessionals (40.3%). This structure changed very little from 2002 to 2007.

During the past three recessions (early 1980s, 1990s, and 2000s) the number of MLS librarians continued to increase, although at a different rate: 3.5 percent, 21.6 percent, and 3.7 percent, respectively. The staff structure remained reasonably consistent over the three recessions. It is noted that staff salaries, measured in constant dollars per capita, increased in the past two recessions based on data from the NCES: 14.4 percent and 4.3 percent, respectively, while other expenditures decreased.

TYPE OF WORK DONE BY MLS LIBRARIANS

An indication of the type of work done by MLS librarians can be seen through the primary areas or departments in which they work. About 7 percent of these librarians said their library was not organized by department, meaning they performed a variety of activities. About an eighth work in administration, but most MLS librarians work in user services or reference and research (55%). Examined by years of experience, those working in administration increased from 4 percent with under 10 years' experience to 23.9% with 20 or more years. The biggest decrease in type of work is reference and research (i.e., 47.8% with under 10 years down to 23.6% with 20 or more years). It is noted that MLS librarians rate satisfaction with the type of work done very highly (i.e., 4.23 average on a 5-point scale with 1 = dissatisfied to 5 = very satisfied). The librarians were asked whether they would choose librarianship if they could choose their careers again (rating: 1= definitely not, 2 = probably not, 3 = unsure, 4 = probably, 5 = definitely). Over three-fourths said they probably or definitely would, and those who said they would reported a very high satisfaction with type of work done (4.40) versus those who would not (3.31).

MLS librarians reported five levels of their employment: library director (6.2% of MLS librarians), assistant or associate director (4.7%), department or branch head (31.4%), other supervisory capacity (12.2%), as staff in a non-supervisory capacity (40.4%), and other (5.1%). The MLS librarians generally move up as they gain experience, although many remain in a non-supervisory capacity even with 20 or more years of experience (28.3%). This is reflected in a low satisfaction rating by MLS librarians with their opportunities for advancement (3.20 average rating, with 1 = dissatisfied to 5 = very satisfied). Similarly, those who probably or definitely would choose librarianship again have a 3.34 satisfaction rating for opportunities for advancement, and those who probably or definitely would not have a very low satisfaction rating of 2.42.

MLS LIBRARIAN SALARIES AND FRINGE BENEFITS

MLS librarian salaries show a wide range, from 11.3 percent making under $30,000 per year to 7.7 percent making $75,000 and above. A higher proportion of female MLS librarians make under $30,000 (12.2% of females vs. 7.5%) and fewer make $75,000 or more (6.3% vs. 14.2%). Examined by years of experience, females make less at all three ranges of experience (under 10 years, 10 to 19 years, 20 or more years), and they make less at all levels of employment. Average satisfaction with salaries is low at 3.30, but surprisingly, female satisfaction with salaries is only slightly lower than their male counterparts. Satisfaction with salaries is also an important factor in whether or not MLS librarians would choose librarianship again. Those who probably or definitely would choose librarianship have an average rating of 3.45, and for those who probably or definitely would not choose librarianship satisfaction drops considerably to 2.36.

MLS librarians appear to receive excellent fringe benefits, including value-added compensation such as employee medical (80% receive these benefits and only 3% pay all themselves), retirement or pension (82% receive and 9% pay all themselves), and so on. Most libraries provide lenient time off (with adequate number of days off, such as 10% of libraries allowing over 60 days of sick leave and 55% allowing over 60 days of accumulated sick leave), and many provide flexible hours (64% of libraries) and compensatory time (63% of libraries), to name a few of many advantages. The fringe benefits received appear to compensate for low salaries. The average satisfaction rating for fringe benefits is not high (3.58) but higher than for salaries (3.30).

CAREER PATHS OF MLS LIBRARIANS

MLS librarians tend to enter the profession at an older age than many other professions. About one-fourth earned their MLS degrees when they were under 25, and 28 percent earned them between ages 25 and 29, but the rest (45%) were 30 years or older. One reason for this is that 38 percent had worked previously in a library in a full-time capacity but not as a librarian, and 35 percent had worked as a professional in another occupation. Over 50 percent of these MLS librarians had worked in these capacities for five or more years. The hiring experience is that three-fourths of the MLS librarians that were hired in 2007 were hired the first year following receipt of their degree, and 93 percent within the subsequent year. This pattern held for librarians with all three levels of years of experience (i.e., under 10 years, 10 to 19 years, and 20 or more years).

Eighty-five percent of the current MLS librarians say they have remained employed in a public library since their initial employment. The rest have moved in and out of public library employment because of illness or disability, work in another occupation, family obligations (e.g., relocation or to raise children), military, to further education, library downsized, and so on. Males tend much more to leave for another occupation or be downsized, while females are more likely to leave for family obligations (although about equally for relocation).

Current MLS librarians report their anticipated age of retirement, and the Library Survey observed the actual age of retirement by those who did in 2007. The age of anticipated retirement is somewhat older than that reported. The anticipated age is similar for males and females, but males tend to actually retire at a younger age. Some current MLS librarians (4%) retired and came back to work in a library, often as temporary or part-time employees, meaning salaries (or wages) and fringe benefits change (to the advantage of the libraries).

TEN-YEAR DEMAND AND SUPPLY FOR MLS LIBRARIANS

A 10-year forecast for MLS librarians is based on three measures. The first is a forecast of the total number expected to be in the workforce over ten years starting in 2007–08 and ending in 2016–17. The second is the attrition that is expected in each year based on an actuarial-like analysis of the age and gender each year and the observed numbers who leave (and sometimes return) due to death, illness, retirement, and other reasons. The number who leave (or return) is subtracted from the previous year. Finally, current vacancies (1,408 in 2007) are added to the workforce in the first year. The total attrition from the beginning workforce (36,169 head count) is 21,165 MLS librarians, the number of vacancies is 1,408, and the expected number of new positions needed over ten years is 3,745 MLS librarians. Therefore, the 10-year demand for new MLS librarians is estimated at 26,318.

It is uncertain what the supply for public MLS librarians is likely to be because public libraries will be competing with other libraries and other organizations that have a need for MLS graduates. The total number of master's degrees awarded from U.S. programs accredited by the ALA has grown somewhat since 1980, but it remained relatively flat through the 1990s and then experienced a burst of growth from 2003 onward.[4] Master's degrees awarded from U.S. ALA-accredited programs in 2009 totaled 7,199.[5] Much of this recent growth has been attributed to the emergence of web-based distance education programs and expansion of ALA accreditation to include a handful of additional master's programs in information science, information management, etc. The IMLS study's 2009 survey of ALA-accredited programs in the United States determined that approximately 5,850 master's degrees were awarded.[6] However, the library workplace faces increasing competition for those graduates, especially from the growing information industry. Individual academic programs estimated that between 49 percent and 96 percent of their graduates take jobs in libraries, resulting in an overall average of 77 percent. This yields an effective supply of approximately 4,500 graduates moving into library positions in 2008–09. Very few degree programs are anticipating growth over the next several years: some are experiencing a slight decline attributed to the economy; a handful are anticipating small increases. We can assume that the supply of qualified librarians will remain steady during the decade.

Thus, based on the 2007 Library Survey including academic, school, and special libraries, the anticipated demand for 62,320 librarians to work in libraries over the next decade cannot be met by the 45,000 graduates expected to take library positions during that time. The unmet demand of 17,320 librarians is the equivalent of almost four times the total annual U.S. supply of librarians into libraries. Two factors exacerbate this deficit in supply: the age at which librarians graduate with their master's degrees, and increased competition for librarians.

ISSUES CONCERNING THE FUTURE OF
THE PUBLIC LIBRARY WORKFORCE

Determining future workforce needs for accredited MLS librarians is a challenging task for several reasons:

- Future workforce needs may not be identical or even similar to current needs.

- With the current recession, projecting workforce needs even in the short term is difficult at best, and especially so with workforce needs in sectors tied closely to the economy.

- Current job conditions, as well as projections about future workforce needs, influence individuals' decisions, thereby altering the future demand/supply ratio.

- Graduate and professional degree recipients not only fill existing workforce needs but go on to shape the workforce, creating new demand and new opportunities for economic growth and social benefits through the jobs they take.

However, despite the difficulty in projecting workforce needs, they are extremely important for the profession and the educational institutions that graduate accredited MLS librarians. We have gathered and analyzed the best information available, but believe strongly that the assumptions and trends will have to be revisited regularly as new information becomes available.

OPERATIONAL ISSUES CONCERNING
PUBLIC LIBRARY COLLECTIONS

It has been shown that circulation increases steadily during normal times and more so during recessions. Below are some issues concerning library collections. The total size of collections of print materials rose from 2002 to 2007 (3.4%) but remained flat in terms of items per capita. Total book purchases declined over the same period (−5.6%) and even more so in purchases per 1,000 population, from 7 in 2002 to 6.3 in 2007 (−10%), while serials purchases decreased some (−6.1% in total purchases and −10% in purchases per 1,000 population for the same period). Both audio and video average collections per library increased substantially during this period: video to 5,030 in 2007 from 3,140 in 2002 (60% in total purchases and 53% per 1,000 population) and audio from 3,910 to 4,980 (27% in total purchases and 22% per 1,000 population).

The 2007 Library Survey showed that periodical and book collections remained primarily in print (over 95% of libraries said less than 25% of their collections are electronic), although 38 percent of libraries said more periodical subscriptions are electronic compared to five years earlier and 53 percent said more books purchased are electronic.

Some licensed databases involve access to electronic materials. Public libraries average a total of 34 such licenses, and nearly all say the number is increasing. About 42 percent of the licenses are obtained through state-sponsored means, and about an equal proportion directly by the libraries or through consortia, and 5 percent are from group networks. About 40 percent of libraries indicate that license negotiation skills are important to their libraries. Part of that is due to the fact that the parent organizations conduct license negotiations for only 20 percent of the libraries.

Total annual collection expenditures increased to $10.2 million in 2007 from about $9.25 million in 2002 (a 10.3% increase). However, in constant dollars per capita, the collection expenditures decreased by 4.8 percent, even in light of increased use of the collections. The average expenditures per library in 2007 (Library Survey) were $101,000 for the print collection; $15,000 for the electronic collection; and $32,000 for other collections. All showed increases compared to five years earlier.

One aspect of such expenditures is that public libraries rely on consortia, networks, and other organizations to support collection purchases and operations. Sixty-six percent say they are members of an average of 3.2 consortia, and 16 percent rely on an average of three contractors or vendors (not including popular vendors such as EBSCO, OCLC, etc.). Consortia provide cooperative purchasing or group discounts, apply for E-rate on behalf of member libraries, support courier or other document delivery services, and enable resource sharing of all types, among many other valuable services. Clearly, these ingenious and generous cooperative activities have helped public libraries in the past and have become ever more essential during recessions.

One indicator of the importance of outside services such as consortia is the extent to which library functions are performed by the library staff or elsewhere. Use of external services is shown to be valuable in terms of staff time and other expenditures. For example, cataloging and preservation of electronic materials, and access to licensed databases and to electronic collections, are all largely done elsewhere. Also, the libraries rely on their parent organizations for some administrative activities such as accounting, finance, personnel, and systems/IT support.

SOME EDUCATION AND TRAINING ISSUES

MLS librarians were asked to rate how well they thought their library and information studies/science (LIS) education prepared them for their initial work assignment and their current position. Ratings were 1 = not at all well to 7 = extremely well. Ratings for the initial assignments were, as might be expected, somewhat higher than for their current position (4.69 vs. 4.31). Ratings for the initial assignment tend to increase by the years of experience of the MLS librarians, but tend to go down for the current position.

Because of the changing library environment and advancement in positions, many public libraries support various types of education and training for their staff. In total the libraries averaged about $7,000 for such support in 2007. Nearly all libraries support attendance at professional meetings at an average of about $2,400, external workshops ($1,500), and internal formal training ($1,400). Some libraries (38%) support evening classes (average of $1,000 per library across all libraries) or virtual university courses (72% of libraries at $450). The trend in expenditures is up in all cases in 2007 compared to five years earlier.

Libraries were asked to report on the importance of competencies for their libraries. Competencies are generally expressed as knowledge, skills, and attitudes or abilities. Altogether, libraries reported on 46 competencies by whether the competency was currently applicable to the library, the rating of its importance to the library (1 = not at all important to 5 = absolutely essential), and the trend in its importance compared to five years earlier.

Some examples of competencies with average ratings over 4.00 and applicable to over 90 percent of libraries are as follows: knowledge of sources of print materials

(4.19, 96%), ability to select and evaluate materials (4.21, 96%), knowledge of circulation principles (4.14, 98%), ability to conduct appropriate reference interviews (4.04, 95%), knowledge/skills to perform online database searches (4.19, 98%), knowledge of user needs and requirements (4.16, 98%), technical knowledge and skills (4.04, 96%), and knowledge of computer operating systems (4.35, 93%).

Management/operations competencies included management knowledge and skills (4.35, 97%), knowledge of planning and budgeting principles (4.41, 95%), skills to develop library policies (4.02, 96%), skills to recruit, interview, and hire personnel (4.08, 93%), knowledge of legal, financial, and funding issues (4.05, 91%), public relations and marketing skills (4.12, 97%), leadership skills (4.31, 98%), and knowledge of funders' expectations of the library (4.10, 93%).

General professional competencies included ability to communicate effectively in writing (4.32, 99%) and orally (4.41, 100%), critical thinking skills for library problems (4.36, 100%), positive attitudes toward users and colleagues (4.60, 100%), and knowledge of behavior management skills, for example, dealing with difficult patrons (4.13, 97%).

The large number of management and administration competencies and their increasing importance to public libraries confirms the tendency for satisfaction with LIS education preparation to be lower for librarians with greater experience as they move into administrative and management positions.

Some competencies for which 75 percent or more libraries indicate that their importance has increased over the previous five years include knowledge of sources of other materials (82%), knowledge and skills to perform online database searches (78%), and web content management skills (77%). Obviously, additional competencies are also important, but not apparently as much as the few highlighted above.

Notes

1. More information is available at www.interconnectionsreport.org.

2. More information is available at www.libraryworkforce.org.

3. The proportion of visits made for various purposes was established in the 2006 Telephone Survey and applied to the IMLS 2007 estimate of the number of in-person visits. A survey of 131 public libraries in 2006 provided estimates of the proportion of visits made by adults, adults who brought children (5 and under), and children (6 to 17). Note that the 126 million visits by children 5 and under are also included in adult visits. Libraries report all purposes of a visit, and the most important purpose on a specific visit. All told, a visit is made for an average of 1.82 purposes.

4. D. M. Davis and T. D. Hall, "Diversity Counts," 2006, American Library Association, www.ala .org/ala/aboutala/offices/diversity/diversitycounts/diversitycounts_rev0.pdf.

5. Data reported to the Association for Library and Information Science Education (ALISE). Note that reported programs included some that were unaccredited at the time of the study.

6. Data from the study survey were collected prior to actual graduation in the academic year 2008–09 and are lower than the numbers later reported to ALISE.

THE STRONG UPWARD TREND IN USE OF PUBLIC LIBRARIES

This chapter provides abundant evidence of the strong positive trend in the use of public libraries in the United States up until 2007. The evidence covers the size of the population served by public libraries and the numbers of visitors, visits, and services provided. The fact that these trends are so positive has important implications for communities' education, personal and family welfare, and workplace productivity and quality, as well as the fulfillment of recreational and entertainment needs. The implications of increased library use for these benefits are demonstrated in chapter 3. More use also increases the economic value of public libraries and the economic return on investment in those libraries, as discussed in chapter 4. It is shown in chapter 9 that the use of public libraries increased during the past two recessions, and recent evidence as well as anecdotal evidence show this may well be true during the current recession. Finally, greater use can affect libraries' operational expenses and staffing patterns, which are discussed in chapters 5 and 6.

Library visits and use increase over time both in total and per capita. Visits are currently made in-person and remotely online. Interestingly, our studies show that a rapid growth in remote online visits apparently has not negatively affected the number of in-person visits and may actually increase them. There appears to be a shift in trends of the extent to which some services are used. Access to Internet services such as search engines (e.g., Google or Yahoo) is used extensively through remote online and through library workstations, which suggests that the Internet does not replace public libraries but may actually support library visits and use. On the other hand, though some services such as circulation are positively affected, trends in the use of other services are dampened, such as reference transactions. Although reference transactions have declined, the complexity of the questions has increased. This may be attributable to the topical databases (e.g., news, business, etc.) available in libraries and to the search engines through the Internet that enable people to address some of their simpler questions.

The evidence of use is based on several sources, including the National Center for Education Statistics now administered by the Institute of Museum and Library Services, and two IMLS-funded projects, including a 2006 National Telephone Survey of adults[1] and 2007 surveys of public libraries and librarians.[2] Finally, the American Library Association has conducted or sponsored a number of studies that provide evidence or that support evidence from these other sources.

POSITIVE TREND IN POPULATION SERVED BY PUBLIC LIBRARIES

Most public libraries are serving an ever-growing population. Data from the NCES (2002) and the IMLS public library surveys (2007) show that the population[3] served per library increased about 7 percent during the time period from 2002 to 2007, due in part to the population growing faster than the number of libraries. The unduplicated population of the library's legal service area increased by about 5.3 percent, but the number of libraries increased by only 0.8 percent. In 2007 a total of 1,222 sampled public libraries in the 2007 Library Survey reported trends in size of population served compared to five years ago. These results support the NCES/IMLS reports of increasing size of population served but also show that some libraries report a decreased population served. Most libraries reported the population size served was up (58%), although 14 percent reported this was down, as shown in table 2.1. The increased population served partially contributes to a trend in the numbers of visitors and visits as described below.

Table 2.1
General Trend in Size of Population Served Compared to Five Years Ago: 2007

| | TREND (%) | | | | |
| | Down | | | Up | |
Sample (n)	>5%	0 to 5%	Flat	0 to 5%	>5%
1,222	3.0	11.0	27.9	33.3	24.7

University of North Carolina at Chapel Hill, School of Information and Library Science, for the Institute of Museum and Library Services

TYPE OF VISIT TO PUBLIC LIBRARIES MADE BY ADULTS

A substantial number of adults (18 and over) visit public libraries in-person and remotely online. In fact, based on the 2006 Telephone Survey of 5,251 completed interviews, it is estimated that 149 million adults visited in-person and 71 million visited remotely online in the past 12 months. Many of these adults had visited both in-person and remotely (42% of visitors), while 54 percent visited only in-person and 4 percent visited remotely only. This has been confirmed in more recent household surveys conducted for the ALA by Harris Interactive and KRC Research (2009 and 2010, respectively), where in-person visitors were estimated at 65 percent (about 151.4 million) of the U.S. population that had used a public library in the last 12 months.

The type of visit made depends on the demographics of visitors (and household income and level of education completed). For example, females are somewhat more likely than males to visit in-person and remotely, and younger adults are more likely to visit in-person and are much more likely to visit remotely. There is little difference in in-person visits among racial and ethnic categories, but the 2006 Telephone Survey indicates that black or African American adults are much less likely to visit remotely. Both higher levels of education and household income have a positive bearing on in-person and remote visits. For details, see text and charts in the Web Extra supplement, available at www.alaeditions.org/webextras/.

POSITIVE TREND IN NUMBER OF VISITS TO PUBLIC LIBRARIES BY ADULTS AND CHILDREN

Not only do many adults visit public libraries in-person and remotely online but, based on the 2006 Telephone Survey (n = 688), they visit them well over 1 billion times annually (i.e., adults visited 849 million times in-person and 622 million times remotely). The ranges of the number of visits are shown in the two pie charts below, and the ALA ranges are also given below, which helps validate the survey results (figures 2.1 and 2.2). Another indicator of the number of visits is found by asking telephone interviewees how long ago their last visit was, as shown in table 2.2. Both questions, number of visits and how long ago the last visit was, indicate a substantial number of visits by adults.

While we do not have exact survey results on the number of visits by children, we have an indication from a 2006 survey of 131 public libraries of the proportion of visits by adults, adults who brought children 5 and under, and children 6 to 17 years of age. These proportions provide estimates of the number of visits by children. For example, parents (or someone else) are said to visit about 126 million times with children 5 and under.[4] It is encouraging and important that parents (or someone) from 80 percent of households with children in this age group brought children to

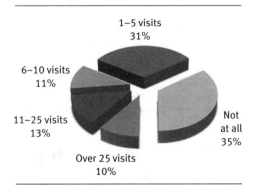

Figure 2.1
Proportion of In-Person Visitors to Public Libraries, by Frequency of Visits: 2006 Telephone Survey (n = 688)

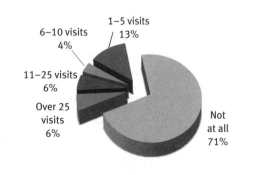

Figure 2.1 (Cont.)
Proportion of Remote Visitors to Public Libraries, by Frequency of Visits: 2006 Telephone Survey (n = 688)

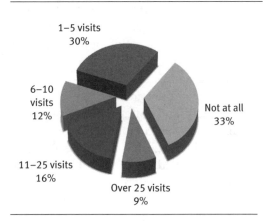

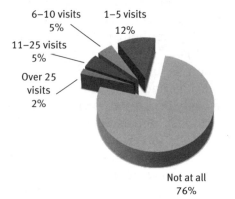

Figure 2.2

Proportion of In-Person Visitors to Public Libraries, by Frequency of Visits: ALA Survey

Figure 2.2 (Cont.)

Proportion of Remote Visitors to Public Libraries, by Frequency of Visits: ALA Survey

Table 2.2

Proportion of In-Person and Remote Online Visits to Public Libraries, by Length of Time since the Last Visit Was Made: Adults (18 and Over) in 2006

When Last Visit Was Made	Proportion of In-Person Visitors (n = 686 (%)	Proportion of Remote Online Visitors (n = 688) (%)
In the last week	23.2	29.0
1 to 2 weeks ago	15.5	15.9
3 to 4 weeks ago	10.2	11.1
1 to 2 months ago	22.6	20.4
3 to 4 months ago	11.2	9.9
Over 4 months ago	17.3	13.7
ALL	100.0	100.0

University of North Carolina at Chapel Hill, School of Information and Library Science, for the Institute of Museum and Library Services

read or check out books for them on 74 million visits in the previous 12 months. Parents in the 2006 Telephone Survey were also asked to report visits by their children ages 6 to 17. An estimated total of 51 million of these children were reported by adults to have visited public libraries in the previous year, mostly for recreation or entertainment purposes (58%) but also to study or complete classroom assignments (50%) or to attend public library aftercare (3%). The reasons for annual visits by these children are given in figure 2.3. While many never visit for those purposes, many of them are frequent visitors. The survey of 131 public libraries produces an estimate of 459 million visits by children aged 6 to 17.

Adults visit public libraries more now than in the past. To establish a trend in the number of visits, in the 2006 Telephone Survey adults were asked if they had visited public libraries more often, less often, or about the same in the past 12 months as done previously. They indicated they visited in-person slightly more often (21.2% of adults more often vs. 20.6% less often). This was reaffirmed in the 2009 ALA Household Survey conducted by KRC Research, which showed an increase in the

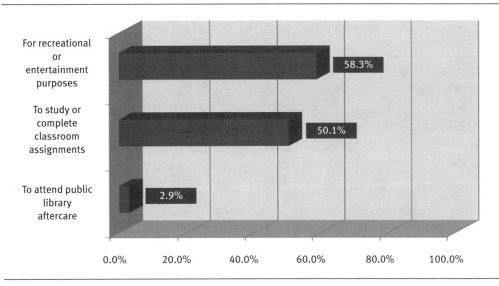

Figure 2.3
Proportion of Children (6 to 17 Years of Age) Who Visited Public Libraries for Various Reasons in 2006 (n = 644)

frequency of visits "over twenty-five times" during the past year as compared with previous years' responses for this visit frequency range. On the other hand, the 2006 Telephone Survey found individuals reported visiting remotely much more often (32.1% more often vs. 13% less often) than in the past.

The NCES/IMLS reports show that in-person visits increased 15.3 percent to 1.434 billion in 2007 from 1.244 billion in 2002. This represents an increase in in-person visits per capita to 4.9 visits from 4.5, or an 8.9 percent increase. The number of children attending children's programs also increased to 58.9 million from 52.1 during this five-year period (i.e., a 13.1% increase). All of this evidence suggests a substantial increase in the number of public library visits.

Over 2,000 public libraries surveyed in the 2007 Library Survey provide additional evidence of the strong positive trend in in-person and remote visits to their libraries. About 77.5 percent of libraries reported that annual in-person visits were up compared to five years ago, while only 12.6 percent said visits were down. Of course, the average visits depend on the number of hours per week that libraries are open. The libraries on average were open 48 hours per week, which resulted in an average of 130,000 annual visits per library or 52 visits per hour.

Referring to the trend (compared to five years ago) in population served (58% of libraries report the trend is up and 14% down), it appears that the positive trend in visits is substantially greater (78% report trend is up, 13% down). Based on the 2007 Library Survey, the trend in in-person visits varies some by the number of in-person visits. Specifically, the higher the overall number of annual visits, the greater the proportional increase over time. For example, about 75 percent of libraries with fewer than 10,000 visits per year report that visits are up and 14 percent report visits are down, while 80 percent of libraries with 250,000 or more visits per year report visits are up and 11 percent are down, as shown in table 2.3. However, table 2.3 shows that when the trend is subdivided into 0 to 5 percent and over 5 percent of visits being up, it is clear that the upward trend in libraries with more annual visits is much higher.

Table 2.3

Total Annual In-Person Visits per Library, and Trend Compared to Five Years Ago, by Range of In-Person Visits: 2007

Range of In-Person Visits (000)	Sample (n)	Visits per Library (000)	TREND (%)				
			Down		Flat	Up	
			>5%	0 to 5%		0 to 5%	>5%
<10	423	4.7	4.0	10.4	10.7	36.6	38.2
10 to 49	631	25.6	5.3	9.7	9.6	29.9	45.6
50 to 249	723	123.4	4.3	6.9	9.2	28.8	50.7
250 or more	341	593.0	3.6	7.1	9.8	26.6	53.0

University of North Carolina at Chapel Hill, School of Information and Library Science, for the Institute of Museum and Library Services

Table 2.4

Total Annual Visits to Library Website per Library, Average per In-Person Visits, and Trend Compared to Five Years Ago, by Range of In-Person Visits: 2007

Range of In-Person Visits (000)	Sample (n)	Website Visits per Library (000)	Website Visits per In-Person Visit	TREND (%)				
				Down		Flat	Up	
				>50%	0 to 50%		0 to 50%	>50%
<10	346	2.0	0.43	7.8	1.6	3.1	46.9	40.6
10 to 49	505	9.7	0.31	1.4	0.7	7.0	38.0	52.8
50 to 249	575	64.8	0.43	2.1	1.3	3.9	31.4	61.2
250 or more	291	953.4	1.73	0.5	2.1	2.1	31.4	63.9

University of North Carolina at Chapel Hill, School of Information and Library Science, for the Institute of Museum and Library Services

A similar pattern exists for website (i.e., remote) and database visits. The average number of website visits is estimated from the 2007 Library Survey to be about 100,000 visits per library annually, or an average of 0.50 visits per in-person visit.[5] However, the trend in the number of website visits is much higher than observed for in-person visits. Ninety-two percent of libraries indicated more remote visits, and only 3 percent said they had fewer visits. The number of website visits also varied somewhat by number of visits, as shown in table 2.4.

Evidence shows that public library visits tend to increase during recessions. For example, in-person visits increased to 820 million from 507 million during the early 1990s recession, or 32.3 percent per capita. During the early 2000s recession in-person visits increased to 1.32 billion from 1.15 billion, or 9.3 percent per capita. A 2009 national Household Survey by KRC Research for the ALA provides some indication of increased visits during the current recession. Comparing findings with the 2006 KRC survey, they found that the average number of in-person visits per visitor increased to 12.7 in 2009 from 9.1 in 2006 (a 40% increase), and average visits by computer increased to 6 from 2.9 during this time period (107% increase), but visits by telephone decreased to 1.1 from 1.5 (−26.7% decrease). Thus, all visits increased 46.7 percent, emphasizing the increased importance of public libraries during recessions. This trend was affirmed in the 2010 Harris Interactive survey.

RELATION OF IN-PERSON AND REMOTE ONLINE VISITS TO PUBLIC LIBRARIES

Results from the 2006 Telephone Survey compare in-person and remote visits. Even though remote visitors average more visits per visitor than in-person visitors do (8.8 in-person visits per remote visitors vs. 5.7 for in-person visitors), there is abundant evidence that remote online visits do not replace in-person visits and might actually increase them some. Only 4 percent of adults who visited by either means did so by remote online only. This suggests that remote use does not replace in-person visits to any extent, which is supported by the evidence given above that in-person trends in visits are not down and in-person visits per capita increased during the 2002–2007 period (based on NCES/IMLS).

There also is evidence from the 2006 Telephone Survey (n = 1,105) that in-person and remote visits by adults are correlated, as shown in figure 2.4. For example, remote online visitors who visited 1 to 5 times in the past year averaged 2.2 in-person visits, and those who visited remotely over 25 times averaged 7.3 in-person visits.

Prior to Internet access to public library services, there was a direct correlation between distance to the library in minutes and the number of visits made annually. That is, the farther away people were from the library, the fewer visits they made. While all necessary data were not obtained in the 2006 Telephone Survey, two recent statewide surveys (Florida and Pennsylvania) show that distance has little bearing these days on the number of visits. Thus, remote online access may have minimized the distance factor, since those located far away may visit remotely now.

Remote online access to public libraries has increased total combined visits dramatically. In 1992 average in-person visits per adult were observed to be 2.76 and had risen to 3.4 visits per adult in 2006, an increase of 23 percent. Yet, in 2006, there were a total combined number of 6 visits per adult when the average of 2.6 remote online visits per adult is added to the in-person visits. Thus, in effect, the average number of visits per adult had increased 117 percent from 1992 to 2006.

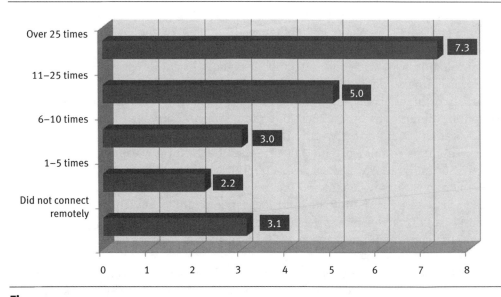

Figure 2.4
Average In-Person Visits to Public Libraries, by Ranges of Number of Remote Online Visits in 2006 (n = 1,105)

The number of remote online visits may increase as general use and the number of users of the Internet increase. Currently, not all public library visitors use the Internet. About 71 percent of adults who use the Internet are also in-person visitors to public libraries, whereas only 47 percent of adults who do not use the Internet are also public library visitors. As suggested above, non-users of the Internet might be inclined to visit public libraries in-person more if they could use the Internet and access libraries remotely online.

It is noted that NCES/IMLS annual public library reports show that the number of bookmobiles decreased to 808 in FY 2007 from 873 in 2002 (−7.4%). This might be caused in part by remote online access. The number of bookmobiles decreased in both previous recessions: from 1,102 to 996 (−9.6%) in the early 1990s and from 884 to 844 (−4.5%) in the early 2000s, probably as a result of cost-cutting actions.

REASONS FOR CHOOSING IN-PERSON AND REMOTE ONLINE VISITS

As part of the 2006 Telephone Survey, adults (n = 688) were asked the reasons they chose to visit the library in-person or remotely online for their last visit. "Because it was convenient or easy to use" was the most frequently mentioned reason for both types of visit, although it was mentioned more often for the remote online visits (94% of remote visitors vs. 82% of in-person visitors). About 70 percent of both types of visits were chosen because the visit did not cost much in time or money. Therefore, in-person visitors appear not to be concerned with the time and cost of traveling to the library, perhaps again because previous longer trips are currently replaced by remote online access.

Somewhat more visitors consider that in-person visits provide the best source of information (76% of in-person visitors vs. 64% of remote visitors). This is confirmed by ratings of importance (1 = low to 5 = high) of the attributes of information obtained from the library. Quality and completeness of information obtained were both rated higher by in-person visitors: that is, an average 4.35 rating by in-person visitors versus 4.20 by remote visitors for quality and 4.26 versus 3.99 for completeness of information. Timeliness, or how up-to-date information was, and how new the information was, were both rated about equally by both types of visitors (about 4.25 for timeliness and 3.80 for how new the information was).

Trustworthiness is an important issue for adults. In fact, in another survey as a non-public library part of the 2006 Telephone Survey, surveyed adults (n = 1,700) rated libraries far more trustworthy than several other information providers (e.g., 4.58 for libraries compared with 3.00, 2.54, and 2.14 for government, commercial, and private individual websites, respectively). Many public library visitors in the 2006 Telephone Survey considered the fact that the information provided could be trusted as a reason for visiting the libraries in-person (66% of visitors) and remotely online (75%). Trustworthiness received the highest rating from among the information attributes mentioned above (4.56 by in-person visitors and 4.48 by remote visitors).

Evidence shows that higher trust in public libraries is achieved through greater use by comparing those who visited 1 to 5 times in-person to those who visited over 5 times in the past 12 months. When asked, "How trustworthy do you consider a library as a source of information (1 = not at all to 5 = extremely trustworthy)," adults who visited over 5 times gave a rating of 4.67 versus 4.34 for those who visited 1 to 5 times. Furthermore, the proportion of visitors who visited because information could be trusted was somewhat higher for the frequent visitors (74% of frequent visitors vs. 65% of all visitors). This pattern also exists for in-person and remote online visitors. This suggests that trust in public libraries is established through experience achieved through use, although people who consider the information *not* trustworthy would not use the library if they didn't need to!

TREND IN USE OF SERVICES PROVIDED BY PUBLIC LIBRARIES

This section deals with evidence of the use of services from four sources: annual public library reports administered by the NCES (2002) and the IMLS (2007), the 2007 Library Survey, and the 2006 Telephone Survey of adults. Most services demonstrate a strong positive trend through 2007, but the recession has thus far had some influence, both positive as well as negative, on services (see chapter 9). The trend in service usage reflects trends in visits and clearly has consequences on library operations (chapter 5), as well as the value and return on investment in public libraries (chapter 4).

The NCES/IMLS annual data show trends in circulation, reference transactions, interlibrary lending and borrowing, children's services, and use of electronic resources. The 2007 Library Survey reports categorization of the level of use[6] and trends in the use of 39 services (presented in detailed tables in the Web Extra supplement, available at www.alaeditions.org/webextras/). The 2006 adult Telephone Survey provides estimates of the proportion of visits during which various services are used.

The NCES/IMLS reports that *circulation* in public libraries increased from 1.90 billion in 2002 to 2.16 billion in FY 2007, or an increase of 13.7 percent. Even taking the increased size of the population into account, the increase is 8.8 percent (i.e., 7.4 items in circulation per capita in 2007, up from 6.8 in 2002). Circulation of children's materials increased 8.3 percent from 682.9 million in 2002 to 739.7 million in 2007. Nearly all 2007 surveyed public libraries indicated that circulation is extensively used (87.5%) or often used (11%). Seventy-two percent of libraries (n = 431) reported that there is more circulation now than five years ago, and only 12.6 percent said less, thus confirming the NCES/IMLS annual data and that the trend holds for most public libraries.

Circulation is observed to increase even more during recessions. For example, during the 1990s and 2000s recessions, circulation increased from 1.39 billion in 1990 to 1.57 billion in 1994, or 12.9 percent in four years, and from 1.71 billion in 2000 to 2.01 billion in 2004 (a 17.5% increase), or 10.3 percent and 10.9 percent increases per capita, respectively.

Surveyed adults reported in 2006 that they checked out one or more books on 63.6 percent of their in-person visits and checked out a video, DVD, CD, or audiotape, including audiobooks, on 25.9 percent of their visits. Although we do not have specific evidence, we believe that remote online access may have contributed to increased circulation where these users request circulated items and then visit the library to pick them up, perhaps on visits combined with visits to other places such as banks, shops, etc. (see chapter 4, where such joint visits are discussed). The adult survey indicated that 56.1 percent of remote visits were made to obtain information from a librarian or the library, which could include circulation requests. Further evidence of remote influence on circulation is that remote access to an online catalog is provided by about 80 percent of libraries, and 54 percent of libraries indicate this service is extensively used; and, moreover, the trend is substantially up (86.6% say the service is used more now than five years ago, and only 2% say less).

Both *interlibrary lending and borrowing* are extensively used, with strong trends upward. The NCES/IMLS annual public library data show that the amount and trend of borrowing and lending are almost equal. The number of interlibrary loans received in 2007 was 49.9 million, up 115 percent from 2002; and considering the population served, the increase was up 103 percent from 84.1 loans per 1,000 population in 2002 to 171.1 loans in 2007. The 2007 Library Survey revealed similar results for borrowing in print and electronic format. Ninety-four percent of libraries say they borrow in print and 31 percent in electronic format. The trend in both formats shows that 60 percent of libraries do interlibrary borrowing more now and about 13 percent less. It may be that use of this service is up because of a downward trend in the size of and expenditure on collections (see chapter 5).

Interlibrary borrowing by public libraries spikes upward during recessions. For example, in the 1990s items borrowed increased to 8.64 from 5.36 million (+61.2%) and in the 2000s to 30.47 from 16.26 million (+87.4%). Considered as items borrowed per 1,000 population, the increases were 58.8 percent and 75.9 percent, respectively. One reason for interlibrary borrowing (and lending) increasing so much is that expenditures on collections decreased substantially during the two recessions: −13.6 percent in constant dollars per capita in the 1990s and −11.4 percent in the 2000s. Anecdotal evidence from press reports of a large number of public libraries indicates that this trend may also hold true during this current recession (see the Web Extra supplement, available at www.alaeditions.org/webextras/).

The trend for *reference services* is very different from that observed for other public library services. The NCES/IMLS reports about 292.4 million reference transactions in 2007 (or 0.97 transactions per capita), down from 301.8 million in 2002 (or 1.08 transactions per capita), representing a 3.1 percent decrease overall and an absolute decline in transactions per capita of 0.10. The public libraries surveyed in 2007 said that general reference and research is extensively used in only 28.9 percent of the libraries, and the trend is mixed. Thirty-four percent of libraries indicate there is more use, but nearly the same proportion say use is less (28%) now than five years ago. About 42 percent of adults from the 2006 Telephone Survey indicated they asked a librarian to help find information in the library or on the Internet from the library workstation on their last in-person visit. The 2007 IMLS data show that about 20 percent of visits involved reference transactions, down from 24 percent in 2002. It may be that access to the Internet in the library, accounting for about 25 percent of visits in FY 2007, has displaced some traditional library reference services. Combined, in-person reference and Internet use represent 45 percent of public library visits reported by the IMLS for FY 2007.

The number of reference transactions increased during the 1990s recession from 209 million in 1990 to 258 million in 1994 (+12.7%), or about +9.8 percent per capita. The reference transactions also increased during the 2000s recession to 304 million in 2004 (+4.5%) from 291 million in 2000, or a small decrease of 1.3 percent when adjusted by population.

Even though many adults surveyed in 2006 said they used *reference materials* in the library (35.6% on the last visit), only 17 percent of libraries report that reference tools are used extensively, and more of the libraries report they are used less now than five years ago (31%) than report they are used more (25%). On the other hand, most libraries in 2007 say that access to an online catalog in the library is used extensively (68%), and the trend in use is definitely up (66% report that use is more now and only 5% indicate less use). This is in line with the trend in circulation.

The NCES/IMLS report a large number of *public-use Internet terminals* available in public libraries and a substantial and increasing use of these terminals. In 2007 there were 207,551 such terminals, or about 12.5 per stationary outlet (i.e., central libraries and branches). This means that there are 3.6 terminals per 5,000 population. The total number of terminals has increased by 66,000 (about 47%) since 2002, and terminals per 5,000 population increased 44 percent since 2002. Most (96%) of the 2007 surveyed libraries report they currently provide user workstations, and these are used extensively in 84 percent of those libraries. The trend is substantial, with 88 percent of the libraries reporting more use now, but only 2 percent less. In 2010 the ALA reported that 99 percent of libraries offered public Internet access and averaged 14.2 public workstations per library outlet.[7]

The 2006 Telephone Survey showed that 73 million adults visited a public library and used a library-provided workstation to access the Internet, use online library resources, or use other services. Thus, about one-third of all adults, and 49 percent of in-person library visitors, used this service. The reasons given for that last use of the service are somewhat similar to the other in-person and remote online visits as follows: it was convenient or easy to use (87% of visits), it was the best source of information (74%), the information could be trusted (58%, somewhat lower than the other two types of visits), and it did not cost much in time or money (58%). A 2010 study conducted by the IMLS and the University of Washington Information School found that about 77 million (45%) of library users are public library Internet users.[8]

The services used by in-person online visitors are given as "any service used," and the "most helpful services" are shown in table 2.5. The dominant service is use of a search engine (e.g., Google or Yahoo), where 70 percent of these visits involve such search engines, and it is the most helpful service used in 45 percent of visits. These users were asked to rate the attributes of the workstations and related services (with 1 being the worst rating and 5 the best). Attributes included hours/days made available (4.14 average rating), software applications (3.92), hardware available (3.89), the number of workstations (3.87), and time allowed per session (3.67). These ratings tend to reflect some concerns over the immediate availability of workstations and the time allowed per session. Limited time per session could have a bearing on the value of the service (see chapter 4). In the 2009–2010 ALA connectivity study, 73.5 percent of libraries reported fewer public Internet workstations than patrons who wished to use them throughout a typical day.

The 2006 Telephone Survey revealed that many in-person visitors *use materials in the library* such as reading a book, magazine, or newspaper in the library (44% last visit) or watching a video or DVD or listening to music in the library (6% of visits). The Library Survey shows that access to the library collections is available in most libraries, but the level of use and the trend in use vary somewhat. The print back files and print current periodicals are available in most libraries (97% and 94%, respectively), but the back files are used more extensively than current print periodicals

Table 2.5

Proportion and Number of In-Person Online Visits to Public Libraries to Obtain Needed Information, by Online Source Used: Adults (18 and Over) in 2006 (n = 259)

In-Person Online Service Used	Proportion of All Uses (%)	Number of Uses (millions)	Proportion of Most Helpful Uses (%)	Number of Uses (millions)
Search engine, e.g., Google or Yahoo	45.1	170	70.3	264
Viewed or downloaded e-books	9.5	36	9.3	35
Viewed or downloaded articles	11.5	43	35.5	133
Viewed a blogger website	0.8	3	18.1	68
Looked at another website	11.5	43	46.3	174
Used e-mail	7.5	28	35.5	133
Used chat mail or instant message	1.2	4	6.6	25
Obtained information from a librarian or the library	11.9	45	52.5	197
Other	1.0	4	5.4	20
All	100.0	376	—	1,049

University of North Carolina at Chapel Hill, School of Information and Library Science, for the Institute of Museum and Library Services

(79% and 30%, respectively). The back files are said to be used more now than in the past (54% of libraries) and less in only 9 percent of libraries. Current print periodicals are used more in 35 percent of libraries and less in 28 percent of them. Thus, the availability of electronic journal/periodical collections may have some impact on the current print periodical use and trend. About 15 percent of libraries provide access to e-journals; even though they are not *extensively* used (6% of libraries), they are used *often* (52%). About 48 percent of libraries indicate this collection is used more (48%) and none say less. Over one-third of visits by adults to use workstations involve viewing or downloading articles from full-text databases, which may also contribute to the diminishing use of current print periodicals.

Clearly public libraries seek to *support patrons with special needs.* Most public libraries provide materials for the visually impaired (80%) and the hearing-impaired (43%), although these materials are not used extensively due to the size of the number of potential users.[9] The trend in use is up some, perhaps due to our aging population (i.e., 38% of libraries say there is more use now for visually impaired and 27% for hearing-impaired). The U.S. Census Bureau's American FactFinder reports in 2008 that about 12 percent of the total civilian non-institutionalized population has a disability. About 38 percent of adults 65 years or older report a disability.

Foreign-language materials are found in 75 percent of libraries, and 42 percent indicate there is more use of them now. About one-third of the libraries provide foreign-language assistance, with 46 percent indicating more use now.

According to the 2006 Telephone Survey, about 6 percent of adult in-person visits involved some kind of *instruction or training* for technology, electronic publications, or traditional bibliographic instruction. The 2007 Library Survey indicates that technology instruction is provided by more libraries than electronic publication or bibliographic instruction (62% vs. 43% and 44%, respectively), has more extensive use (13% vs. 4% and 9%), and more libraries have more use now than in the past (50% vs. 48% and 28%). Undoubtedly, the increased use of user workstations and access to the Internet and electronic publications have a bearing on these results.

Library meeting rooms are well used. Adults surveyed in the 2006 Telephone Survey said they attended a meeting organized by others than the library, and used a library meeting room for this purpose on about 10 percent of their last visits. About 9 percent of last visits involved attending *a lecture or some other sort of program,* and NCES/IMLS public library data indicate that children's program attendance was 58.9 million in 2007, up 13.1 percent from 2002. The 2010 ALA Household Survey reported that 45 percent of Americans said they take their children to the library because of the great programs and services, and 41 percent said they attend story hour and other such programs at the library.

Aside from reference transactions, the use of library services appears to increase substantially during recessions. The current recession has demonstrated a particular increase in supporting job seeking and providing access to government information and services (see chapter 9).

It is abundantly clear that public libraries serve an ever-increasing population with services relevant to their changing information needs and use of technologies. The wide range of purposes for which users visit public libraries and their use of so many services are described in the next chapter.

Notes

1. José-Marie Griffiths and Donald W. King, "Interconnections: The IMLS National Study on the Use of Libraries, Museums and the Internet: Public Library Report," 2008, available at www.bryant.edu/interconnectionsreport/.
2. "A National Study of the Future of Public Librarians in the Workforce," 2009, available at www.bryant.edu/libraryworkforce/.
3. NCES and IMLS report the population served in three ways in FY 2007:

   ▪ official stated population—300,008 million in FY 2007

   ▪ population of legal service area (i.e., the number of people in the geographic area for which a public library had been established to offer services and from which the library derives revenue)—295,539 million in FY 2007

   ▪ unduplicated population of legal area (i.e., total unduplicated population of those areas in the state that receive library services)—292,029 million in FY 2007

4. The 126 million visits are duplicated in the 849 million times adults visited in-person, since at least two persons are involved in these visits.
5. Note that the 2006 Telephone Survey of adults yielded estimates of 849 million in-person and 622 million remote online visits, or 0.73 remote visits per in-person visit.
6. Level of use was categorized by being (1) core, extensively used; (2) core, often used; and (3) secondary provision and used.
7. American Library Association, "Libraries Connect Communities: Public Library Funding & Technology Access Study, 2009–2010," 2010, available at www.ala.org/plinternetfunding.
8. U.S. IMPACT Study, "Opportunity for All: How the American Public Benefits from Internet Access at U.S. Libraries," 2010, available at http://tacha.washington.edu/usimpact.
9. U.S. Census Bureau, American FactFinder, http://factfinder.census.gov/servlet/ADP Table?_bm=y&-geo_id=01000US&-ds_name=ACS_2008_1YR_G00_&-_lang=en&-_caller =geoselect&-format=.

PUBLIC LIBRARIES ARE USED FOR MANY PURPOSES

Books, magazines, newspapers, and other information sources are often used for recreation or entertainment. However, they are also frequently used by adults to address important situations in which information is needed to make a decision or solve a problem. Part of the 2006 Telephone Survey (n = 1,843) asked adults about the last time they encountered such situations and to describe them. Those situations were post-classified into about 200 categories, grouped by personal or family, education, lifelong learning, and work-related information needs. Estimates are made for the number of occurrences and the proportion of information sources (e.g., books, persons, Internet, etc.) that are most helpful in addressing these needs.

It is useful for librarians to know all the information sources used by potential users and the relative proportion of use of those sources made in public and other libraries. It is also beneficial to observe how the different sources and library use change over time. Such results can serve as a baseline for future longitudinal studies. We examine the role that public and other libraries, in particular, play in providing information sources that satisfy various information needs as well as recreation and entertainment purposes. This provides a general context for the use of public libraries and the purposes for which public libraries are used. An understanding of these purposes also provides the background for assessing the value of public library services and the return on investment in them described in chapter 4.

As mentioned in chapter 2, public libraries can be visited in-person or remotely online. This chapter also demonstrates that public libraries are used for many varied purposes. In-person visits involve a wide variety of purposes. Since workstations are used for online activities rather than for other in-person services, the purposes of these two types of visits are distinguished below as *in-person online visits* and *other in-person visits.* The numerous purposes for which public libraries are used are discussed in detail below for these two types of in-person and remote online visits, following discussion of the context of public library use.

ADULTS CHOOSE FROM AMONG MANY POSSIBLE SOURCES AND RELY ON PUBLIC LIBRARIES TO PROVIDE THESE SOURCES

Information users are always faced with making choices as to which *sources* of information to use (i.e., books, the Internet, family or colleagues, etc.) and which *providers* of the sources to use (e.g., purchase books or use the library; use the Internet from home, office, or library; etc.). The 2006 Telephone Survey addressed these choices by asking the following *critical incident* question: "I'd like you to think about the last important situation where you needed information. The situation may be personal-, family-, education-, or work-related. By focusing on the last important information need, we can learn more about where people get information and how useful it is. I'm going to ask several details about this last important situation where you needed information." The question leads to an indication of how libraries in general and public libraries specifically are used to address various situations and the role played by them from among the many sources and providers of information that might be used by adults. Chapter 2 provided an indication of why public library services were chosen.

Public library visitors and other information users have the option of using a variety of sources for addressing important situations. The 2006 Telephone Survey asked which sources and providers were used for the last situation and which were most helpful. On average, adults used about 2.6 sources for each situation. Table 3.1 is a list of such sources/providers with the proportion (%) of situations in which they were used and which were most helpful.

It is clear that adults rely on many sources and providers of information for addressing important situations. The Internet is used for about one-third of situations addressed, yet is most helpful in over half of the situations (52%). Library providers are used for about 11 percent of situations addressed, with 8 percent of occurrences being most helpful. Yet in the next chapter we show that libraries provide sources of information that have extensive value to their users. Also, since there are remote online visits to public libraries, some Internet use from home and at work or school may include these remote visits. The survey did not provide this distinction.

It is estimated[1] that there were about 29.2 billion annual occurrences in 2006 of personal or family information needs (n = 1,109). The most frequent personal or family information need related to health or wellness (39% of these needs), followed by finance or legal needs (19%), getting information about travel or vacation (8%), to make a purchase or sell something (8%), support a hobby or work around the house (5%), address death-related issues such as wills, funeral arrangements, etc. (3%), job hunting or career planning (2%), and so on are shown in figure 3.1. (For details, see the text and charts in the Web Extra supplement, available at www.alaeditions.org/webextras/.) The sources of information which are most helpful in addressing these needs are shown in figure 3.1. Clearly the Internet is typically the most frequent

Table 3.1

List of Sources and Providers of Information Used to Address an Important Situation (n = 1,843)

	LAST SITUATION	
Sources and Providers	**Used (%)**	**Most Helpful (%)**
Family members	29.0	7.6
Friends or colleagues	42.4	11.0
One's own or a family member's newspaper or magazine	16.8	1.8
Newspaper/magazine from library	5.9	0.6
Newspaper/magazine from elsewhere	4.6	0.6
One's own or a family member's book	16.6	4.9
Books from a library	17.2	5.3
Books from elsewhere	7.6	2.0
Internet at home	52.2	31.6
Internet at work or school	27.1	17.0
Internet at a library	5.2	1.8
Internet from somewhere else	2.7	1.3
Television	6.7	0.6
A museum	1.7	0.3
Some other source/provider	22.9	13.6
TOTAL	258.6	100.0

University of North Carolina at Chapel Hill, School of Information and Library Science, for the Institute of Museum and Library Services

source used, with persons (e.g., family, friends, colleagues, and professionals such as doctors, lawyers, etc.) the second most frequent, followed by publications.

The 12.4 billion education information needs observed in 2006 fall into two general groups: (1) formal education that involves adult student information needs (4.6 billion occurrences), teacher information needs, including homeschooling (5.4 billion) and adults helping children with homework or other queries (0.5 billion); and (2) other information needs about schools, education requirements, etc. (0.9 billion), about counseling, PTA, etc. (0.6 billion), and other education information needs (0.4 billion).

Work-related information needs account for about 27.7 billion occurrences, including work in specific businesses such as law firms, accounting firms, medical practices, etc., or small organizations such as retail businesses, hospitals, farms, churches, etc. Needs include research in medicine, science, engineering, legal issues, legislation, etc. (28%); administration such as personnel, accounting or finance, budgeting, facilities, etc. (19%); marketing or sales (10%); general information needs such as looking up addresses, locating someone or a business, travel arrangements, etc. (10%); specific kinds of work such as computing, systems, software, purchasing, repairs, etc. (8%); and work involving specific kinds of businesses such as law firms, accountants, realtors, travel agents, farms, etc. (25%). Sources include the Internet (67%), person (18%), books (8%), newspapers/magazines (3%), and other (5%).

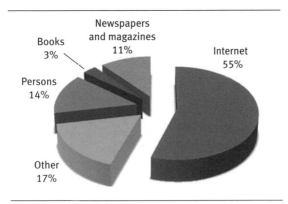

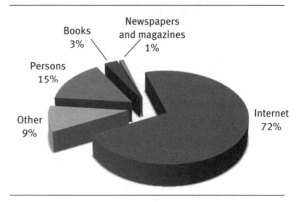

Figure 3.1
Proportion of Situations in Which Source Is the
Most Helpful in Addressing Purchase or Sales
Information Needs

Figure 3.1 (Cont.)
Proportion of Situations in Which Source Is the
Most Helpful in Addressing Travel or Vacation
Information Needs

Again the Internet is by far the most frequent source used in the workplace, followed by persons.

Since the Internet is the most frequent source used to address most important situations, the 2006 Telephone Survey (n = 1,280) specifically addressed Internet use.[2] Internet use shows that 83 percent of adults use it, and total annual use in 2006 was estimated to be about 100 billion, with 34 billion of these uses addressed to important situations described above.[3] The question, then, is how often libraries are used by adults to access the Internet to address important situations. Figures 3.2 and 3.3 show the proportion of places where adults have used the Internet, including libraries and their type. Clearly public libraries play a significant role in Internet use. A 2010 study from the IMLS, conducted by the University of Washington, estimates that 77 million Americans fourteen years or older are using public libraries to access the Internet.[4] The next section examines the many purposes of use related to public library remote online visits and in-person online visits.

About 22 percent of books that are read are obtained from a library, and 64 percent of the library books are from public libraries. Book readers were asked about the last book read for addressing an important situation and where the book was obtained. (Note that these readings do not include those for recreation and entertainment.) Most said it was their own or a family member's (44%), but one-third said it was from a library. Seventy percent of public library visitors said the purpose was for personal or family needs, with 19 percent for work-related needs and 11 percent for education or lifelong learning needs. Across all purposes of reading, 72 percent of the last readings by public library visitors are for recreation or entertainment, 21 percent for personal or family purposes, 28 percent for educational needs, and 8 percent for work-related needs, recognizing that a book can be read for multiple purposes. Non-public library visitors read books for much the same purposes as public library visitors.

Publications are also important sources for addressing important situations and for recreation and entertainment. Below we examine the relative role libraries play in providing books, magazines, trade and scholarly journals, and newspapers and the purposes for which these publications are read. The 2006 Telephone Survey shows that public library visitors[5] are much more likely than non-visitors to read

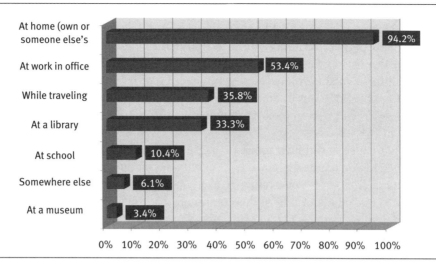

Figure 3.2
Places Where Adult Users Have Used the Internet in 2006 (n = 1,280)

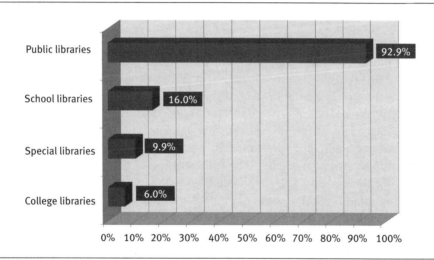

Figure 3.3
Types of Libraries Where the Internet Is Used (% of Users)

each of these types of publications and read more of them. For example, 89 percent of public library visitors said they had read from any part of a book (chapter or section) in the past 12 months while only 69 percent of non-visitors had, and the public library visitors averaged reading from 22 books versus 14 by non-visitors. Furthermore, the public library visitors are much more likely to read from electronic versions of publications. For example, 25 percent of the readings of journals by public library visitors are in electronic format versus 19 percent by non-visitors.

Adults were asked how many newspapers they normally read, and 79 percent said they normally read an average of 1.5 newspapers. They were asked where they obtained the last newspaper that was read. Most (63%) read from personal subscriptions, newsstands (23%), or other places such as a doctor's office (9%). Only one percent of newspapers are read in libraries, of which 66 percent are in public libraries. About 9 percent of public library users read the last newspaper in electronic format versus 5 percent of non-visitors. A 2009 study shows that print newspaper reading is still most prevalent.[6] Most readings by public library visitors are for general local, national, or international news (95% of reading), recreation or entertainment (69%), sports (57%), or financial information (47%). Non-public library visitors are less likely to read newspapers for financial information (37%) or recreation or entertainment (61%).

Adults were also asked how many magazines they read regularly (not including professional trade or scholarly journals). Seventy-seven percent said they read regularly from magazines, and they average reading regularly from three such magazines. They were also asked about where they obtained the last magazine read. Most were from personal subscriptions (72%) and newsstands (14%). About 2.4 percent were read in a library, of which 55 percent were in public libraries. About 2.6 percent of reading by public library visitors was in electronic format versus 1.5 percent for non-visitors. Most reading of magazines by public library users was for recreation or entertainment (68%), to keep current (43%), for a hobby or work around the house (37%), for health or wellness (29%), and shopping, travel, etc. (23%), recognizing that the last reading can involve several purposes. Here non-public library visitors are somewhat less likely to read magazines for personal or family health (24%) and for shopping, travel, etc. (19%).

Nearly one-fourth of adults said they have ever read from a professional trade or professional journal. They were asked to indicate information about where they obtained the last journal they read (including titles they read infrequently such as those found in an online search). About half were from personal subscriptions and 10 percent from an author or colleague. About one-third were from a library, including those obtained from the Internet or a web search (21%) or other library copy (12%). Of those, 23 percent were found in public libraries, but most were obtained from academic or special libraries. The topics of the last journal read were science or engineering such as physics, social sciences, etc. (23%), medicine such as health care, nursing, etc. (21%), business or management including finance, advertising, etc. (20%), arts or humanities (9%), education or teaching, English teachers, general education, etc. (8%), law (21%), and non-professional topics such as aircraft mechanics, truck driving, quilting, etc. (25%). Over half (55%) of non-public library visitors read about non-professional topics. The comparisons indicate the importance of public libraries in professional reading.

TREND IN PURPOSES OF PUBLIC LIBRARY USE

Four national telephone surveys were conducted for the ALA in 2002, 2006, 2009, and 2010. In-person, telephone, or computer visitors were asked: "Thinking back over the last year, which one of the following did you use the public library for?" The results are given in table 3.2. Entertainment and educational purposes dominate in all years and may be an indicator that the current recession results in users relying on libraries more and borrowing rather than purchasing. The increase in circulation supports this assertion.

These purposes of use are about the same as established in the 2006 Telephone Survey. However, adults were asked about their last visit, all of the purposes of that

Table 3.2

Purposes for Which the Public Library Was Most Used in the Last Year: 2002, 2006, 2009, 2010

Most Uses	OVERALL (%)			
	2002 (n = 658)	2006 (n = 703)	2009 (n = 604)	2010 (n = 663)
Educational purposes (for homework or to take a class)	35	32	28	41
Entertainment	26	26	35	35
To use a computer	n/a	n/a	n/a	17
U.S. or local news or information	4	5	2	11
To conduct a job search or write a résumé	3	5	3	11
Information on health issues	4	6	6	6
Meet up with friends	n/a	2	5	5
Financial or investment news or information	3	3	3	3

American Library Association. Household surveys conducted by KRC Research (2002, 2006, 2009) and Harris Interactive (2010).

last visit, and the most important of these purposes. These results are given for the three types of visits and give a little more detail on the purpose of visits as explained in the section below.

PURPOSES OF PUBLIC LIBRARY VISITS AND SERVICE USE

The purposes of in-person visits vary substantially by whether the visit involves online use of the library's workstation or the use of other services, and therefore a distinction is made for these two types of visits, referred to as *in-person online visits* and *other in-person visits*. The third type of visit is remote online. As indicated in chapter 2, there were 849 million in-person visits and 622 million remote online visits made by adults in 2006. Each visit can involve multiple uses of the library services. For example, there are 1.66 such uses per in-person visit and 1.94 uses per remote online visit. The total number of uses is given in table 3.3 by type of visit and purposes of use.

Table 3.3

Total Use of Public Library Services, by Type of Visit and Purposes of Use: 2006 (n = 2,037)

Purpose of Use	TYPES OF VISIT (Uses in Millions)			
	Other In-Person	In-Person Online	Remote Online	Total
Recreation/entertainment	596	53	148	797
Personal/family needs	266	90	264	620
Educational	330	150	454	934
Work-related	76	83	169	328
Total	1,268	376	1,035	2,679

University of North Carolina at Chapel Hill, School of Information and Library Science, for the Institute of Museum and Library Services

About 1.471 billion "most important" visits were made to public libraries, with 28.9 percent for recreation or entertainment purposes, 23.2 percent for meeting personal or family needs, 35.3 percent for educational purposes, and 12.6 percent for meeting work-related needs. Many of these uses were confirmed in the January 2010 ALA Household Survey, where 29 percent reported use for educational purposes and 23 percent for entertainment. It is clear that public libraries are used for many important purposes.

Public library visits for educational purposes are made about equally by white and black or African American adults (about 30% of visits) and are slightly higher for Hispanic adults (35%). Black or African American adults visit much less frequently for recreation or entertainment needs than the other two groups (17% vs. 24% and 35%), and white Americans tend to visit less for work-related needs (15% vs. 24% and 27%). The visits do not differ much in purpose of visit based on age, gender, or education levels, with the exception that older adults visit more for recreation or entertainment and less for work-related needs, as one would expect. (See related figures in the Web Extra supplement, available at www.alaeditions.org/webextras/.)

PURPOSES OF OTHER IN-PERSON VISITS

Visits and service use are often for several purposes. Considering all purposes for other in-person uses, about 47 percent are made for recreation or entertainment, 21 pecent to meet personal or family needs, 26 percent for educational needs, and 6 percent for work-related needs. The range of purposes for these uses is impressive, as shown below.

About 596 million other in-person visits are made annually for *recreation or entertainment* purposes. These purposes were achieved by reading in the library (84% of these visits), listening to music or other recordings (16%), watching a movie or other program (14%), or attending a lecture or other such program (9%). These visitors say they have benefited in many ways from these activities, citing that they encouraged further reading, viewing, or listening (77% of these visits), helped learn something new (55%), broadened their perspective on life (41%), inspired them (41%), and so on.

Personal or family information purposes are satisfied through about 266 million other in-person visits. These purposes fulfilled a variety of such needs, including helping with a hobby or learning how to fix something (32% of these visits), finding out about health or wellness issues (18%), addressing an occasional need such as purchasing a home or automobile or planning a vacation (13%) keeping up with the news or current events (13%), and so on.

About 330 million other in-person visits are made for *educational* purposes. These involve small children ages 5 and under (7% of these visits), students aged 6 to 17 to study or complete classroom assignments (52%), students aged 18 or over to research a topic of interest, work on an assignment, use as a place of study, or keep up with the literature (3%), teachers for their own continued learning, to keep up with the literature, to prepare for a class lecture, or to prepare a lecture (6%), and adults to continue learning or perform personal research (31%). Clearly public libraries play an essential role in education. Also, in the next chapter on public library value and return on investment, it is shown that public libraries serve school and academic libraries in various ways such as through interlibrary lending, and they also serve homeschooled children.

Finally, other in-person uses provide substantial support to businesses and other organizations through satisfying *work-related* purposes. About 76 million visits are made for this purpose for research (77% of these uses); marketing or sales, financial or tax issues, or legal issues (14% each) and administration or operational issues (9% each). In a 2009–2010 study of public libraries prepared by the ALA, it was estimated that about 88 percent of them provide access to jobs databases and other job opportunity resources, 75 percent to civil service exam materials, and 69 percent to software and other resources to help patrons create résumés and other employment materials. Sixty-seven percent of public libraries report helping patrons complete online job applications.[7]

NUMBER OF IN-PERSON ONLINE AND REMOTE ONLINE VISITS AND SOURCES USED

The 2006 Telephone Survey provides some details of the last in-person online visits (n = 259) and remote online visits (n = 98). The estimated number of in-person online visits is about 194 million and remote online 622 million. Thus, there are about three times as many remote online visits as in-person online visits. The sources used during online uses include search engines (e.g., Google or Yahoo), obtaining information from a librarian or library, looking at a non-library website, visiting a blogger website, viewing or downloading an electronic article or book, and using e-mail or using chat mail or instant messaging. Remote online visits average 3.6 sources used per visit versus 2.8 sources for in-person online visits, and the time spent per visit is somewhat higher for remote online (63 vs. 29 minutes per visit). In chapter 2 it was shown that there are some time restrictions on workstations which are used for in-person online visits.

The source most frequently used on the last online visit is a search engine (70.3% and 78.6% of visits, respectively, for in-person online and remote online). Obtaining information from a library or librarian is a frequently used source for both types of visits (52.5% and 56.1% of visits for in-person and remote online). Remote online visits may include requests for circulated items, as suggested in chapter 2, but are not distinguished in the survey. Viewing or downloading electronic articles and books is done more often on remote online visits than on in-person visits (i.e., 50% vs. 35.5% for articles and 15.3% vs. 9.3% for books). This may be because in-person visitors have access to materials in the library and users don't need to obtain them electronically. Many more remote online visits than in-person visits involve using e-mail (68.4% vs. 35.5% of visits), using chat mail or instant messaging (15.3% vs. 6.6% of visits), and viewing a blogger website (24.5% vs. 18.1% of visits). Viewing non-library websites is roughly the same for both types of visits (about 47%). The disparity in sources used is not reflected in the purposes of use, as shown below.

PURPOSES OF USE FOR IN-PERSON ONLINE AND REMOTE ONLINE VISITS

There is remarkably little difference in purposes of use related to the two types of online visits (see table 3.4). Education needs are clearly the most dominant use (39.7% and 43.9% of visits for in-person and remote, respectively), with recreation

Table 3.4

Purposes of In-Person Online and Remote Online Visits to Public
Libraries: 2006 (n = 262, n = 101)

| | TYPE OF ONLINE VISIT | |
| | In-Person | Remote |
Most Important Purpose of Use	(%)	(%)
Recreation/entertainment	13.7	14.3
Personal/family needs	24.4	25.5
Education needs	39.7	43.9
Work-related needs	22.2	16.3
All	100.0	100.0
Total Visits (in millions)	204	561

*University of North Carolina at Chapel Hill, School of Information and Library Science,
for the Institute of Museum and Library Services*

and entertainment the least (13.7% and 14.3%) and work-related (22.2% and 16.3%, respectively) in between. Thus, both types of visits are used for answering specific information needs and may have greater impact on the libraries' value and return on investment, as shown in chapter 4.

Notes

1. José-Marie Griffiths and Donald W. King, "Interconnections: The IMLS National Study on the Use of Libraries, Museums and the Internet: General Information Report," 2008, available at www.bryant.edu/interconnectionsreport/.

2. Ibid.

3. Note: Internet use has tripled in a decade; see this report dated 2009: www.census.gov/Press-Release/www/releases/archives/communication_industries/013849.html.

4. Institute of Museum and Library Services, "Opportunity for All: How the American Public Benefits from Internet Access at U.S. Libraries," 2010. This report and its appendixes are available at http://tascha.washington.edu/usimpact.

5. Public library visitors are those who have visited a public library in the past 12 months.

6. Martin Langeveld, "Print Is Still King: Only 3% of Newspaper Reading Happens Online," Nieman Journalism Lab, available at www.niemanlab.org/2009/04/print-is-still-king-only-3-percent-of-newspaper-reading-actually-happens-online/.

7. American Library Association, "Libraries Connect Communities: Public Library Funding & Technology Access Study 2009–2010," 2010, available at www.ala.org/plinternetfunding.

THE VALUE OF PUBLIC LIBRARIES AND TAXPAYER RETURN ON INVESTMENT

Chapter 2 provided evidence of the number of public library visitors and visits, where visits are categorized by in-person visits (including in-person online visits and visits involving other services) and remote online visits. Discussion of the value of public libraries similarly includes these three types of visits. Economists define two types of *value* of products and services:

> *purchase or exchange value:* what one is willing to pay in time and/or money for use of a product or service

> *use value:* the favorable consequences derived from use of a product or service

The *purchase value* paid by public library users includes the time spent by them in traveling to and from the library and the time spent using the services. The money spent using public library services include travel and parking for in-person visits and the Internet cost of remote online visits. The national total purchase value is established from estimates of the total number of visits given in chapter 2 from the 2006 Telephone Survey. One reason why public library users choose the public library from among the many possible sources of information is that "it did not cost much in time or money," also discussed in chapter 2 for in-person and remote online visits.

The *use value* depends somewhat on the purposes for which public library services are used, as discussed in chapter 3. In this chapter, *use value* is presented in terms of the outcomes of using services such as whether or not needed information was obtained, how well the information addressed needs, whether the use led to a favorable outcome, and whether any time or money was saved from use of the information provided. Another aspect of the outcome is the quality, timeliness, trustworthiness, etc., of information provided by the services. The use of services also led to other providers (e.g., government agencies, other types of libraries, stores, people, museums), which can be considered another important type of favorable outcome.

Yet another aspect of the value of public library services is *contingent valuation,* which is an economic method used to assess the benefits of non-priced goods and services such as those provided by public libraries. This value is achieved by examining the implications of not having public library services. In this chapter contingent value is determined by asking adults about their last visit and "If you did not have access to the library resources or services, what would you have done?" Some adults say they would use another source, in which instance the cost in time or money to use another source is determined when appropriate. The current cost to users is subtracted from the cost to use another source to estimate the contingent value of the service. The contingent value results are based on the 2006 Telephone Survey.

The taxpayer return on investment (ROI) discussed here is based on two statewide studies in Florida in 2004 and in Pennsylvania in 2006. (Web Extra describes ROI, how it is determined, and why it is important.) *Investment* is the sum of federal, state, and local contributions to public libraries. Contingent value involving users is one component of the *return.* However, public libraries also serve school, academic, and special libraries, and a contingent value is also determined for these public library *users.* If public libraries were closed or not in communities, the wages and salaries as well as local purchases would be lost to a community's economy. In-library purchases may come from hosted gift shops, vending machines, photocopiers, etc. In addition, library visitors often use nearby shops, restaurants, and other services before or after their trip to the library. Some revenue to those services would be lost if there were no public library (referred to by us as a *halo* effect). These are all economic contributions to the return on investment. (See www.alaeditions.org/webextras/ for an ROI calculator based on an in-person survey conducted by libraries.)

Public libraries cause an economic ripple effect that increases *gross regional product* (GRP),[1] wages, and jobs. An economic input-output model is used to estimate the input of public libraries on other economic sectors over time. This extends the economic analysis beyond actual users of public libraries to a set of direct, indirect, and induced effects of libraries.

PURCHASE VALUE OF PUBLIC LIBRARIES

As mentioned above, *purchase value* is what public library visitors pay for services in their time going to and from libraries and the time they spend in them. They travel to libraries in many ways such as walking or biking, driving, or taking public transportation or taxis. Some of these modes of transportation cost money, such as for traveling by car, fares, and parking fees. Some cost may be incurred for photocopying as well. Remote and in-person online visitors pay mostly in their time, although there is some, but unknown, cost of using the Internet. It is noted that some library visits involve shared travel to shops, restaurants, banks, etc. The travel costs are adjusted downward to take these visits into account; travel time is also allocated to other in-person and in-person online visits. Travel time is estimated from the two statewide ROI studies.

These average costs per visit are summarized in table 4.1 by type of visit based on visitor surveys. (See www.alaeditions.org/webextras/ for descriptions of detailed calculations.) The cost of time is based on the reported salaries or wages of adults in the

Table 4.1

Average Purchase Value per Visit, by Time and/or Other Cost and by Type of Visit: 2006

	Other In-Person Visits	In-Person Online Visits	Remote Online Visits	All Visits
Time in library or online	52	29	63	53
Time traveling (min)	17	5	—	9
Total time (min)	69	34	63	62
Cost of time	$19.50	$ 9.60	$17.80	$17.45
Travel cost ($)				
Drive	$ 1.40	$ 0.40	—	$ 0.70
Park	$ 0.08	$ 0.02	—	$ 0.05
Other transportation	$ 0.04	$ 0.01	—	$ 0.02
Total travel cost ($)	$ 1.50	$ 0.43	—	$ 0.77
Total cost	$21.00	$10.00	$17.80	$18.20

University of North Carolina at Chapel Hill, School of Information and Library Science, for the Institute of Museum and Library Services

Table 4.2

Average Purchase Value per Visit, by In-Person and Remote Online Visits and by Purpose of Use: 2006 (n = 1,128)

Purpose of Use	In-Person Visits	Remote Online Visits
Recreation and entertainment		
Cost per visit	$18.30	$19.40
Personal or family needs	$23.60	$18.40
Educational needs		
Adult students	$ 6.20	$ 6.30
Teacher	$35.10	$43.20
Adult accompanying a child	$ 5.00	—
Retirees lifelong learning	$16.70	$15.80
Work-related needs	$42.00	$30.70

University of North Carolina at Chapel Hill, School of Information and Library Science, for the Institute of Museum and Library Services

location of the study. The *purchase value,* which ranges from $10 to $21 per visit, demonstrates that visitors are willing to pay substantially for visits. The total annual costs for these visits in 2006 were $13.8 billion for other in-person visits, $1.9 billion for in-person online visits, and $11.10 billion for remote online visits, for a total of about $27 billion. In 2007 the IMLS reported annual library expenditures to be $8 billion. Therefore, visitors actually pay over three times what public libraries actually expend, which is an indicator of the large value to public library communities.

The purchase value varies substantially by the purpose of use, as shown in table 4.2 from a 2006 statewide telephone survey (n = 1,128) in Pennsylvania. These purchase values include both users' time and the other costs associated with travel, etc., estimated in the same manner as above. In-person visits include both other in-person and in-person online visits. The results are adjusted to reflect 2006 Telephone Survey totals of the number of visits by purpose of use.

The differences in purchase values among purposes of use largely reflect the time spent during the visits made for various purposes, but perhaps even more so the value of the specific visitors' time. For example, teachers' purchase value is substantially higher than that of adult students, as a result of disparities in salary or wages and because the number of visits is higher (see chapter 3). Similarly, the work-related users probably include many professionals' salaries. Retirees generally do not receive salaries, but some do have substantial annual incomes. Later in the chapter some reasons are given for the disparities in these values.

USE VALUE OF PUBLIC LIBRARIES

Use value is measured in terms of the outcomes or impact of using public library services. The 2006 Telephone Survey and two statewide surveys (Florida in 2004 and Pennsylvania in 2006) present ample evidence of the extensive value these services provide. This evidence includes statements of the benefits of using the services for recreational or entertainment purposes; the positive attributes of information obtained for personal or family, education, or work-related information needs; how important the services are in meeting the information needs; and other outcomes. One important use value is measured by *contingent valuation,* which indicates how much more it would cost users to obtain needed information if public libraries were not available to adults. Similarly, public libraries serve school, academic, and special libraries, and savings to them are also discussed here. The contingent valuation estimates serve as one component of the return aspect of return on investment.

USE VALUE ACHIEVED FOR OTHER IN-PERSON, IN-PERSON ONLINE, AND REMOTE ONLINE VISITS

In the 2006 Telephone Survey adults were asked to rate attributes of the information they received from the three types of visits (ratings from 1 = worst rating to 5 = best rating). The results of these ratings for five attributes are discussed as follows:

Trustworthiness of the information: this attribute is rated by far the highest of the attributes at 4.52 (4.62 other in-person, 4.35 in-person online, 4.48 remote online). The importance of trust is discussed further in chapter 2.

Quality of information obtained: second-highest attribute at 4.29 (4.34, 4.38, 4.20 by type of visit).

Timeliness or how up-to-date the information was: third highest at 4.26 (4.25, 4.39, 4.23).

Completeness of information obtained: fourth highest at 4.15 (4.27, 4.21, 3.99).

Novelty or how *new* the information was to the user: this information is rated the lowest for all types of visits at 3.80 (3.74, 3.86, 3.85). However, it is not necessarily bad that users knew about information prior to obtaining it, because they may want to confirm what they knew or elaborate on the information.

Further clarification of use value is given below.

Adults were also asked how well the information addressed the reason for their visit. The proportion of visits in which the visitor indicated the reason was completely satisfied was similar for the three types of visits (i.e., about 63% for other in-person, 62% for in-person online, and only 58% for remote online). The adults were also asked to describe the outcome of use as to whether they got all, some, or did not get the information sought. These results varied substantially among the three types of services (i.e., 58% of other in-person visitors said they got all the information vs. 50% for in-person online and 39% for remote online). Clearly, the online services are not as good as the other in-person capabilities. All three services were said to result in a favorable outcome by about 94 percent of visitors, although about one-fourth of in-person online visitors and one-third of remote online visitors said they received too much information. Adults rated the *importance of information* they obtained in meeting information needs, with remote online visits rating the highest at 4.21 compared with about 4.12 for the two in-person types of visits.

Another type of use value is that the visits led to other important sources of information or providers, including other libraries, publications (e.g., articles, books, etc.), the Internet, other persons (e.g., family members, colleagues, doctors, lawyers, etc.), and organizations (e.g., government agency, store, museum, etc.). The visits most frequently led to publications (i.e., 30% of visits leading mostly to books). Libraries were reported as other providers in 26 percent of the visits, with most being other in-person visits leading to other public libraries. The Internet came up for 17 percent of visits, with online visits being the predominant type. About 14 percent of visits led to organizations (mostly government agencies), and 4 percent of visits led to persons (mostly professionals).

THE CONTINGENT VALUE OF THE THREE SERVICES

Contingent valuation is an economic method of evaluating non-priced goods and services (such as those provided by public libraries) that looks at the implications of not having the services. To apply this method the 2006 Telephone Survey respondents (n = 627) were asked, with regard to their last visit to a public library, to indicate what they would do if they did not have access to the library to obtain the needed service or information. They were given the option of reporting:

- would not bother to do anything
- need the information but do not know where else to go for it
- would get the information from another source

The responses were similar for all three types of visits: they would get the information from another source 85–86 percent of the time, they need the information but don't know where else to go for it about 7–9 percent of the time, and they would not bother to do anything else 6–7 percent of the time.

For the majority of instances for which respondents indicated they would get the information from another source, they indicated the type of alternative source they would use. Most remote online visitors would use the parent public library (53% of visits) or another type of library (11%), a person (10%), Internet (10%), organization (5%), or bookstore, etc. (11%) as an alternative source. In-person online visitors are most likely to use other in-library services (24%) or another type of library (18%).

Some say they would use another computer such as at home, work, or belonging to someone else (14%). Many would go to another person (18%) or get publications from other sources (15%). Other in-person visitors would most often go to a bookstore (including Amazon.com, etc.) or rental store (28% of visits). They would sometimes go to another library (14%) or consult with a person (16%), and are twice as likely to go to an organization (government agency, store, or museum) than other visitors (10% vs. 5%).

AMOUNT OF TIME THAT WOULD BE SPENT USING THE ALTERNATIVE SOURCES

Earlier, the time spent using public library services was discussed, and the average time spent per visit was shown to be 63 minutes per remote online visit, 34 minutes per in-person online visit, and 69 minutes per other in-person visit, including both time in the library and traveling.

The time that would be spent accessing and using alternative sources is much larger in all cases: 2.32 hours versus 63 minutes on average for remote online visit alternatives; 1.23 hours versus 34 minutes for in-person online visit alternatives; and 1.40 hours versus 69 minutes for other in-person visit alternatives. A significant proportion of all alternative sources would require spending more than one hour accessing and using them: 64 percent of remote online alternatives, and 38 percent for both in-person online and other in-person alternatives.

The average additional time necessary to access and use an alternative source is 76 minutes for remote online visits, 40 minutes for in-person online visits, and 15 minutes for other in-person visits, or about 1.08 billion hours total.

NET BENEFITS OF REMOTE ONLINE, IN-PERSON ONLINE, AND OTHER IN-PERSON VISITS TO PUBLIC LIBRARIES

There is a cost to use public library services, which includes the time spent going to and from the library, the cost to drive to the library and park, or the cost to take other forms of transportation to and from the library. If there were no public libraries, many visitors say they would use alternative sources to obtain needed information, including the transportation costs to visit those sources and the cost of purchasing or renting from the alternative sources. The net benefit of having public libraries is that visitors save about 640 million hours in their time and $32.6 billion in other costs.

Contingent value or *net benefit* is the total cost to use alternative sources less the current cost to use the public libraries by the three types of visits. Total cost to use alternative sources (less the) current cost to use the public libraries by the three types of visits = contingent value (or "net benefit").

SAVINGS ACHIEVED FROM USE OF INFORMATION OBTAINED DURING REMOTE ONLINE, IN-PERSON ONLINE, AND OTHER IN-PERSON VISITS TO PUBLIC LIBRARIES

In addition to the net benefit resulting from the availability of public libraries, visitors can derive benefit from the information they obtain through use of the public libraries. The information could save time for research, work around the house, travel, etc. The information could also lead to monetary savings by identifying less costly options for purchasing, eliminating the need to hire someone to help, reduce the materials needed, etc.

The survey respondents indicated that if there were no public library, they would sometimes need the information obtained but would not know where to go for it. In these instances, the savings that would have been derived would be lost to the visitor (*lost savings*). In some cases they would not bother to go elsewhere and would therefore not derive any savings. Finally, in some cases, they would achieve no savings at all from the information accessed. The number of visits in which time savings were achieved was 217,800 visits and 249,000 visits for monetary savings. The lost time savings would occur on 38,100 visits and lost monetary savings on 18,800 visits. The total savings achieved for the information obtained from public libraries in 2006 was 2.5 million hours and $154 million. The savings that would be lost if public libraries did not exist was 204,000 hours and $12 million.

USE VALUE OF PUBLIC LIBRARY SERVICES TO OTHER LIBRARIES

Public libraries also serve school, academic, and special libraries by lending them books and other materials, providing searches to online databases licensed by them, and performing other reference services. These organization libraries are said to respect the uniqueness of public library collections, the support from their staff, and the efficiency and reliability of services. The results in table 4.3 present the average use and savings from a 2006 statewide study of 338 libraries in Pennsylvania.

Table 4.3
Annual Average Savings per School, Academic, or Special Library from Use of Public Library Services in Pennsylvania: 2006 (n = 225)

	Number of Libraries	Annual Average Public Library Use per Library	Annual Average Savings per Library ($)
School libraries	3,700	96	$ 900.00
Academic libraries	206	58	$4,850.00
Special libraries	475	81	$1,050.00
Total	4,381	93	$1,100.00

University of North Carolina at Chapel Hill, School of Information and Library Science, for the Institute of Museum and Library Services

Projection to national totals of libraries indicates that public libraries might save school libraries as much as $87 million, academic libraries $18 million, and special libraries $10 million, or about $115 million total. Of course, cooperative arrangements mean these libraries also save public libraries substantially as well (see chapter 5 for a discussion of cooperative arrangements).

The top five public library services used by school libraries include borrowed books (95% of school libraries), used reference services (53% of libraries), borrowed videotapes (52%), borrowed audiobooks (41%), and access to the Internet (39%). School libraries obtained an average of about 65 documents per library, and occasionally used public library meeting-room facilities. The top five reasons why school libraries use public libraries are

- ease of use (55% of libraries)
- depth and breadth of public library collection (52%)
- unique items in collection (39%)
- support for library staff (37%)
- efficiency/speed of service (37%)

The *purchase value* for school libraries is that they average about 41 hours in staff time using public library services.

The top five services used by academic libraries include borrowed books (86% of libraries), obtained photocopies of publications (50%), used reference services (50%), borrowed DVDs, videotapes, and audiobooks (32% each), and searched/copied information from commercially licensed online databases and electronic publications (27%).

The top five reasons why public library services are used by academic libraries include

- unique items in collection (74%)
- ease of use (68%)
- efficiency/speed of service (47%)
- cheaper to use than other alternatives (42%)
- support from library staff (37%)

The *purchase value* for academic libraries is that they average 49 hours of staff time using public library services.

A total of 669 special libraries were identified in Pennsylvania that serve businesses, government, hospitals, and other organizations. A survey of these libraries indicates that about 475 of them (about 71%) have used public library services in the past year. The top five services used include borrowed books (82% of libraries), used reference services (65%), obtained photocopies of articles (53%), searched or obtained information from licensed online databases (41%), and borrowed videotapes (32%).

The top five reasons why public library services are used by special libraries are

- unique items in the collection (58%)
- ease of use (53%)
- depth and breadth of collection (44%)

- cheaper to use than other alternatives (42%)
- support from public library staff (41%)

The *purchase value* for special libraries is that an average of 37 hours of staff time is spent using these public library services.

USE VALUE FROM RECREATION OR ENTERTAINMENT VISITS

An estimated 336 million in-person visits were made nationally in 2006 for recreation or entertainment needs. These needs are met by reading (84% of visits), listening to music or other recordings (16%), watching a movie or other program (14%), and attending a lecture or other such program (9%). The favorable outcomes of these activities include encouraging further reading, viewing, or listening reported for 77 percent of uses, as shown in table 4.4. These outcomes are substantial and contribute to quality of life in many ways.

Table 4.4
Proportion of Other In-Person Visits, by Ways Information or Services Were Helpful in Meeting Recreational or Entertainment Needs: 2006 (n = 152)

Encouraged further reading, viewing, or listening	77%
Helped learn something new	55%
Inspiring	41%
Broadened perspective on life	41%
Led to other interests	28%
Resulted in new way of thinking	24%

University of North Carolina at Chapel Hill, School of Information and Library Science, for the Institute of Museum and Library Services

In a 2010 ALA Household Survey, 77 percent of adult Americans reported borrowing books (e-books, paper books, or audiobooks) from the library, and 35 percent (53 million) visited the library for entertainment needs.

The telephone interviews in Florida (n = 1,128) provide evidence of the contingent value of about $10 per visit (i.e., the cost necessary to use alternative sources if there were no library less the current cost of visits).[2] (Detailed calculations are provided in the Web Extra supplement, available at www.alaeditions.org/webextras/.)

USE VALUE FROM SATISFYING PERSONAL OR FAMILY INFORMATION NEEDS

There were estimated to be 183 million in-person service visits made for personal or family-related information needs in 2006. The top five personal or family information needs include helping with

- a hobby or how to fix something—31% of visits
- health or wellness—18%

- news or current events—13%
- an occasional information need (e.g., planning a vacation)—13%
- culture or religion—10%

Job opportunities were examined in about 3 percent of uses. The ALA 2010 Household Survey found that 17 million Americans (17%) visited their public library to conduct a job search or write a résumé (11%), which reflects the current recession.

The Florida statewide telephone interviews revealed that the contingent value of visits for addressing personal or family-related information needs is $13.70, about the same as this value for recreational or entertainment needs. In addition, the lost value from not knowing where to go if there were no public library is about $0.70 or $14.40 total per visit (i.e., $13.70 plus $0.70).

USE VALUE FROM EDUCATION INFORMATION NEEDS

There are about 246 million in-person visits made by adults for educational purposes. Perhaps this purpose should be called lifelong learning because it includes accompanying a child for this purpose (13% of most important education purpose) and adult continued learning (54% of this purpose). The purposes of adult student in-person uses include as a place to study (38% of uses) and to work on an assignment (63%). Adult student visitors (18 years and over) are in high school (17%), undergraduates (59%), graduate students (14%), or others, such as attending a technical school (10%). Teachers' uses are to prepare for a class or lecture (43% of uses), prepare a paper (7%), and for their own continued learning (86%), of which some is as a student (14% of continued learning uses) and in general (79%).

The Florida statewide studies showed that the total education contingent value is $26.60 per visit with about $2.00 for lost value, for a total value of $28.60. The value for students is $4.30 per visit and $24.00 per visit for teachers, which is slightly less than that for work-related visits.

USE VALUE FROM WORK-RELATED USES

There are 84 million in-person visits made for meeting work-related information needs. Based on the 2006 Telephone Survey (n = 516), these include the following types of visitors: self-employed (17%), from a small business under 50 employees (17%), a large business with 50 employees or more (39%), a government agency (10%), a hospital or health care provider (7%), and other (10%). The types of job-related information needs include for research (63% of work-related visits), to locate a person or organization (35%), financial matters or taxes (17%), legal issues (15%), marketing or sales (18%), management (12%), and operations (8%). Other outcomes of the use of library-provided information include increased productivity (62% of work-related uses), improved work (57%), and savings in time (62%) and money (52%).

The Florida contingent value results for the work-related visits is $29.60 per visit, and the savings from not knowing where to go for information is about $2.60 per use, resulting in a total value of $32.20.

TAXPAYER RETURN ON INVESTMENT IN PUBLIC LIBRARIES

The contingent value of public library services is only one source of the return component of the return on investment. In fact, communities benefit from salaries and wages of public library employees through paid local taxes and goods and services purchased in the community. These and other returns are discussed below, and are based on results from a statewide study conducted in Pennsylvania in 2006 (based on a combination of 1,128 telephone interviews and 2,614 in-library responses).

If there were no public libraries, current users would be affected in various ways. To determine how they would be affected, we asked in-person and remote online visitors what they would do to obtain the information they got from their last use. Some said they would not bother to do anything. Some said they needed the information, but did not know where else to go to obtain it. Others said they would use another source such as a store, another person, academic libraries, etc. We then asked the latter users what sources they would use to get the information and about how much of their time and money they thought it would take to use this source. The estimated cost to use alternative sources was found to be $47.70 per visit. This compares with the $19.80 per visit that public library users currently spend in their time and money using public libraries.

In 2006 it cost public library users $27.90 per visit more to obtain needed or desired information if there were no public libraries (i.e., net benefit). Note that these values are much higher than mentioned above by purpose of visit, since a visit often includes multiple purposes and uses.

Keeping costs fixed in 2006 dollars, increased overall public library use in Pennsylvania in 2008 indicates the alternative sources cost could be $29.80 per visit.

Some information obtained from public libraries saves users time and money such as in performing work, making household repairs, or purchasing a product at a lower price. When such information is needed, but users do not know where else to go, they would lose the savings provided by such information.

In 2006 library users would have lost $2.40 per visit by not knowing where to go to obtain needed information.

In addition to extensive additional costs to users, the local economy would suffer because the library staff's wages and salaries are lost to the economy, and in-state library purchases of publications and other goods and services are lost as well.[3] In 2006

▌ library wages and salaries lost to the economy were $5.20 per visit

▌ library in-state purchases lost to the economy amounted to $2.00 per visit

The public libraries host gift shops, vending machines, copying machines, and other services that are operated by non-library vendors and others. The revenue of these services would also be lost to the local communities. The extent of this loss to the economy is about $0.03 per visit.

Library visitors often use local shops, restaurants, and other services before or after their trip to the library. Some revenue to these services (i.e., a *halo* effect) would be lost if there were no public libraries. Based on a late 1990s study in the United Kingdom, about 23 percent of the total revenue is likely to be lost to the local

Pennsylvania communities. The lost halo effect is estimated to be $2.30 per visit in Pennsylvania.

If there were no public libraries in Pennsylvania, the total economic loss to users and the local economy is estimated to be $41.70 per adult visit. Pennsylvania taxpayers contributed $7.20 per visit in 2006 to public libraries through local, state, and federal taxes. Thus, the 2006 Pennsylvania taxpayer return on investment in public libraries is 5.8 to 1 ($41.70 ÷ $7.20 per visit).[4]

REMI ESTIMATE OF RETURN ON INVESTMENT

Pennsylvania public libraries cause an economic ripple effect that increases gross regional product, wages, and jobs. An economic input-output model (REMI)[5] provides a means of estimating the impact of public libraries on other economic sectors over time. This extends economic analysis beyond actual users of the libraries to a set of direct, indirect, and induced effects of the libraries.

Results are that the GRP increases by $3.79 per dollar of public funding for public libraries, and there is a net impact of $3.14 of GRP per dollar of funding.

Notes

1. Gross regional product is an indicator of the economic well-being of an area (state) measured in terms of the total economic output (analogous to the gross national product).

2. Sometimes Pennsylvania data are used and other times Florida data are used, since analysis of data varied between the two states.

3. Dr. Charles Roddie (Research Fellow, Nuffield College, Oxford) contends that a normal cost-benefit analysis would ignore the "wages and salaries and purchase dollar" component of ROI and, therefore, they are included in error. Personal communication, February 3, 2011.

4. The cost to users is based on a dollar value of their time. The literature concerning the value of time value varies a great deal. Some say that the basis could be the median income of users. Using this approach the ROI would be 5.5 to 1. We chose to refine the value of time of persons having different purposes of use: personal, work-related, teaching, student use, and so on, which yielded 5.8 to 1 ROI.

5. Regional Economic Models, Inc. (REMI) is an integrated input-output and economic model that was specifically used for the two statewide ROI studies (Florida and Pennsylvania). It traces linkages among industry purchases and sales and forecasts future changes in business costs, prices, wages, taxes, etc.

PUBLIC LIBRARY OPERATIONS

This chapter discusses the trends (2002–2007) in public library collections, revenues and expenditures, functions performed in and out of libraries, importance of competencies, and support of education and training. Results are based on the 2007 Library Survey, past NCES and IMLS public library data (2002 and 2007, respectively), and recent ALA reports. Some evidence is provided on the implications of past and current recessions for collections, revenues, and expenditures.

TREND IN PUBLIC LIBRARY COLLECTION SIZE AND PURCHASES

Based on NCES (2002) and IMLS (2007) data, the five-year trend in the size of print collections is up 3.4 percent from 785 million items in 2002 to 812 million in 2007, although remaining the same in terms of items per capita at 2.8. Results from the 2007 Library Survey show that periodical purchases are down some while book purchases are well up.

Average numbers of periodical and book purchases are given in table 5.1, as reported in the 2007 Library Survey. The average number of unique periodical titles purchased per library is estimated to be 202 titles based on the Library Survey. The five-year trend in periodical purchases tends to be down: 39 percent of libraries indicate the number of purchases is down, 35 percent flat, and only 27 percent up. Periodical purchases may be down due to increased access to full-text databases. The NCES and IMLS data seem to confirm these results in that the IMLS reported an average of about 200 subscriptions per library in 2007. They also reported 1.84 million purchases in 2007, down from 1.95 million in 2002 (i.e., a 5.6% decrease), and they

Table 5.1

Number of Unique Periodical Titles Subscribed to and Total Annual Book Purchases
per Library, and Trend Compared to Five Years Ago: 2007

Type of Purchase	Sample (n)	Average Purchases per Library	TREND (%)				
			Less		Same Now	*More*	
			Much	Somewhat		Somewhat	Much
Periodical titles	345	202	13.0	25.5	34.8	20.8	5.9
Books	296	8,500	5.4	13.5	28.9	34.5	18.3

University of North Carolina at Chapel Hill, School of Information and Library Science, for the Institute of Museum and Library Services

Table 5.2

Number of Unique Periodical Titles Subscribed to per Library, and Trend Compared
to Five Years Ago, by Range of In-Person Visits: 2007

Range of Visits (000)	Sample (n)	Periodical Subscriptions per Library	TREND (%)				
			Less		Same Now	*More*	
			Much	Somewhat		Somewhat	Much
<10	65	29	5.1	16.9	57.6	18.6	1.7
10 to 49	96	68	7.5	23.7	38.7	23.7	6.2
50 to 249	116	235	13.8	26.7	26.7	25.0	7.7
250 or more	68	499	27.1	34.3	21.4	11.4	5.7

University of North Carolina at Chapel Hill, School of Information and Library Science, for the Institute of Museum and Library Services

report a decrease in the number of purchases per 1,000 population from 7 in 2002 to 6.3 in 2007 (i.e., a 10% decrease).

On the other hand, there are about 8,500 book purchases per library, and they appear to increase from 2002 to 2007: 19 percent of libraries report a decrease in book purchases, 28 percent are flat, and 53 percent are up. The increase in book purchases may be influenced by the observation that circulation is extensively used in most libraries and the five-year trend is dramatically up: 13 percent less, 16 percent the same, and 71 percent up (see chapter 2). A January 2010 ALA Household Survey reveals that 77 percent of households borrowed books (e-books or books on paper or tape/CD) in the past year. Of households with children, 86 percent reported checking out books, movies, and music as the most important reason they take their children to the library.[1] Table 5.2 gives periodical purchases by range in number of annual in-person visits. These results show that the trend in purchases may decline as the number of in-person visits increase, particularly for libraries with 250,000 or more visits.

Book purchases by range in number of annual in-person visits are shown in table 5.3. In this case, the trend in book purchases tends also to decline some with increased numbers of in-person visits.

The Library Survey results (table 5.4) show the reported proportion of periodical subscriptions and book purchases that are in electronic format. Nearly all

Table 5.3
Total Annual Book Purchases per Library, and Trend Compared to Five Years Ago,
by Range of In-Person Visits: 2007

Range of Visits Visits (000)	Sample (n)	Purchase per Library	TREND (%)				
			Less		Same Now	*More*	
			Much	Somewhat		Somewhat	Much
‹10	61	386	2.1	14.6	25.0	37.5	20.8
10 to 49	86	1,671	5.6	10.1	29.2	38.2	16.9
50 to 249	98	4,330	5.8	12.5	27.9	32.7	21.2
250 or more	51	34,213	8.0	20.0	32.0	28.0	12.0

University of North Carolina at Chapel Hill, School of Information and Library Science, for the Institute of Museum and Library Services

Table 5.4
Proportion (%) of Periodical Subscriptions and Book Purchases That Are Electronic, and Trend Compared
to Five Years Ago: 2007

Range of Visits (000)	Sample (n)	*Proportion (%) Electronic*					TREND (%)				
		0 to 25%	26 to 50%	51 to 75%	76 to 99%	100%	*Less*		Same Now	*More*	
							Much	Somewhat		Somewhat	Much
Periodical subscriptions	366	95.1	1.3	1.1	2.2	0.3	1.0	3.9	57.1	23.9	14.1
Books	342	98.9	0.8	—	0.3	—	5.5	12.2	29.0	35.4	18.0

University of North Carolina at Chapel Hill, School of Information and Library Science, for the Institute of Museum and Library Services

public libraries (95%) infrequently purchase periodicals that are in electronic format (0 to 25% of their purchases), although some 2.5 percent of libraries have predominantly electronic purchases (76% or more of the subscriptions). The five-year trend in electronic periodical purchases is increasing: 5 percent purchasing less, 57 percent the same, and 38 percent more. An even higher proportion of libraries (99%) infrequently purchase books in electronic format (0 to 25% of books purchased) and rarely purchase most of their books in electronic format (0.3% of libraries purchase 76% or more in electronic format). The five-year trend in electronic book purchases is up substantially as well: 18 percent less, 29 percent the same, and 53 percent more. In fact, the 2007 IMLS data show that there are about 157,000 electronic serials found in public libraries, or 17 per library, and 13 million electronic books, or 1,400 per library.

The collections of other materials also increased substantially. The IMLS data show that public libraries held about 46 million audio materials in 2007, up from 36 million in 2002 (a 27.8% increase). The amounts per 1,000 population were 157 in 2007 and 129 per 1,000 population in 2002 (a 21.7% increase). Video collections increased to 46 million in 2007 from 29 million in 2002 (up 58.6%), and there was a 52.9 percent increase in the number of such items per 1,000 population (i.e., 159 from 104 per 1,000 population).

PUBLIC LIBRARY LICENSED DATABASES

The IMLS 2007 data show 387,000 databases in public libraries, or about 42 per library. On the other hand, the 2007 Library Survey estimated 34 licensed databases purchased per library (table 5.5).

Very few public libraries report a decline in the number of database licenses over the past five years (2.6%). Most are the same (17.8%) or have more licenses (79.6%). Libraries vary in the means used to obtain their licenses: 41.5 percent of licenses are obtained through state-sponsored means, about an equal proportion are obtained directly by the library (27.5%) or through consortia (26.1%), and only 4.9 percent are from a group network. Generally, the trend is for somewhat more purchased licensed databases in libraries that have more in-person visits (table 5.6). It may be that the larger libraries have relatively more electronic publications, so the trend in licensed databases is much higher.

The source of licenses varies drastically by range of in-person visits (table 5.7). Libraries with fewer in-person visits tend to rely more on state-sponsored acquisition, whereas those with more in-person visits negotiate for database licenses directly. About an equal proportion of the libraries of all sizes rely on consortia as a source. More information about the impact of networks, cooperatives, and consortia on public libraries appears later in this chapter.

Table 5.5
Number of Licensed Databases Purchased per Library, and Trend Compared to Five Years Ago: 2007

| | | TREND (%) | | | | |
| | | *Less* | | Same | *More* | |
Sample (n)	Database per Library	Much	Somewhat	Now	Somewhat	Much
374	34.0	0.2	2.4	17.8	28.5	51.1

University of North Carolina at Chapel Hill, School of Information and Library Science, for the Institute of Museum and Library Services

Table 5.6
Number of Licensed Databases per Library, and Trend Compared to Five Years Ago, by Range of In-Person Visits: 2007

| | | Number of Licensed Databases per Library | Trend (%) | | | | |
| | | | *Less* | | Same | *More* | |
Range of Visits (000)	Sample (n)		Much	Somewhat	Now	Somewhat	Much
<10	62	12.1	—	2.3	31.8	40.9	28.0
10 to 49	93	20.7	1.3	5.2	28.6	39.0	26.0
50 to 249	117	26.0	—	2.6	16.7	43.0	37.7
250 or more	72	44.9	—	2.9	7.2	27.5	62.3

University of North Carolina at Chapel Hill, School of Information and Library Science, for the Institute of Museum and Library Services

Table 5.7
Proportion (%) of Database Licenses Obtained by Various Means,
by Range of In-Person Visits: 2007

| Range of Visits (000) | Total | MEANS OF OBTAINING DATABASE LICENSE (%) | | | |
		Direct by Library	Through Consortia	Group Networked	State-Sponsored
<10	12.1	5.6	31.0	6.3	57.1
10 to 49	20.7	6.3	21.0	2.4	70.2
50 to 249	26.0	24.8	25.5	3.1	46.5
250 or more	44.9	46.3	27.5	7.0	19.2

University of North Carolina at Chapel Hill, School of Information and Library Science, for the Institute of Museum and Library Services

TREND IN PUBLIC LIBRARY REVENUE

Public library revenue increased in constant dollars (CPI) by about 7.7 percent in 2007 from 2002 based on the NCES and IMLS. However, there was a dramatic shift in the sources of revenue during that time. Federal revenues decreased 13.3 percent in constant dollars to $48 million in 2007; state revenues decreased even more (down 36.3%) to $766 million; local sources made up most of the difference, with an increase of 15.1 percent to $9.25 billion; and other sources also helped with an increase of 7.7 percent to $962 million.

A fairly similar revenue picture occurred during the last two recessions (early 1990s and 2000s), particularly regarding the sources of revenue. The total revenue increased 21.8 percent during the 1990s recession and 29.9 percent during the early 2000s recession. Considering population growth (5.4%) and inflation during the 1990–1994 recession, the total increase in operating income per capita increased only 1.8 percent, reflecting almost exclusively local sources (5.5% increase), while state funding decreased by 10.4 percent, federal by 13 percent, and other sources by 4.4 percent. The 2000–2004 recession exhibited even greater disparity: population growth (+5.8%), total income per capita (−1.9%), local (+3.8%), state (−23.5%), federal (−28.6%), and other funding (−16.5%).

An ALA report[2] provides evidence of funding during the current recession. As part of the "Public Library Funding & Technology Access Study," the ALA surveyed the 51 chief officers of state library agencies in late 2009. The study found:

> Twenty-four states reported cuts in state funding for public libraries between FY 2009 and FY 2010. Of these, nearly half indicated the cuts were greater than 11 percent—almost four times the number that this was the case in the previous year at the state level frequently were compounded by cuts at the local level and cuts in the state library agency budget. When considering current local funding to public libraries, a majority of state libraries reported decreases in the five-to-ten percent range. Seventeen states (37 percent) reported they believed a majority of libraries in their states had received cuts in funding in FY 2010, compared with FY 2009.

It appears that the current recession (2008 and beyond) may be worse for public library funding, particularly if the recession extends beyond four years as some project.

TREND IN PUBLIC LIBRARY EXPENDITURES

The NCES (2002) and IMLS (2007) provide evidence of the trend in expenditures, with comparisons made in constant dollars (CPI). Total expenditures were up 10.3 percent to $10,206 million in 2007 from 2002 and 4.7 percent in constant dollars per capita to $34.95 in 2007 (table 5.8). Staff salaries and wages dominate the expenditures at nearly two-thirds and an increase of 11.7 percent. On the other hand, collection expenditures account for 13.2 percent of expenditures, but they increased less than one percent from 2002 in constant dollars and actually decreased 4.8 percent in constant dollar expenditures per capita. The remaining expenditures (e.g., "other expenditures" that include technology, programs, facilities maintenance, and utilities, etc.) also had increases similar to those of salaries and wages.

The Library Survey produced somewhat different estimates, as given in table 5.9. The average total expenditures per library are estimated to be $1,393,000 versus about $1,100,000 reported by the IMLS. The big difference is in salaries and wages, at $917,000 per library from the Library Survey versus about $730,000 reported by the IMLS. The trend reported by the Library Survey is also much higher.[3] The IMLS reported total expenditures to be $10,206 million in 2007 compared with $8,024 million in 2002. This is a 27.2 percent increase compared with 8 percent of libraries reporting the trend is down, 12 percent flat, and 80 percent up reported in the Library Survey.

The trend in total expenditures, considering range in number of annual in-person visits, is given in table 5.10. Larger libraries, indicated by the number of in-person visits, tend to have a higher positive five-year trend (>10%) in total expenditures (i.e., 41.7% vs. 21.1% for the smallest libraries). There is a tendency for the average total expenditure per visit to be less for larger libraries, perhaps due to economies of scale in their operations.

Average expenditures per library for salaries and wages are $917,000 per library, or 65.8 percent of all expenditures (see table 5.9 for comparison with IMLS, which is 65.5%). The five-year trend in salaries and wages is the most positive of all other individual expenditures, with 5 percent of libraries reporting these expenditures

Table 5.8
Total Annual and Per-Capita Expenditures by Type in 2007, and Change (%) in Constant Dollars from 2002

	EXPENDITURES (2007)			
Type of Expenditure	All ($Millions)	Change (%)	Per Capita ($)	Change (%)
Total	$10,206	+10.3	$34.95	+4.9
Staff	$ 6,685	+11.7	$22.91	+6.1
Collection	$ 1,347	+0.7	$ 4.59	−4.8
Other	$ 2,147	+12.4	$ 7.45	+6.8

NCES, "Public Libraries in the United States FY2002," 2005

IMLS, "Public Libraries Survey FY2007," 2009

University of North Carolina at Chapel Hill, School of Information and Library Science, for the Institute of Museum and Library Services

Table 5.9
Annual Expenditures per Library by Type of Expenditure, and Trend Compared to Five Years Ago: 2007

| Type of Expenditure | Sample (n) | $ per Library (000) | TREND (%) | | | | |
| | | | Down | | | Up | |
			>10%	0 to 10%	Flat	0 to 10%	>10%
Total	1,848	$1,393	2.2	5.8	12.2	47.8	32.0
Salaries and wages	1,834	$ 917	1.5	3.9	10.1	53.4	31.0
Other	—	$ 476	—	—	—	—	—

| | Sample (n) | $ per Library (000) | Less | | Same Now | More | |
			Much	Somewhat		Somewhat	Much
Print collection	324	$ 101	5.9	13.2	22.9	46.9	11.1
Electronic collection	308	$ 15	3.5	4.4	34.8	30.8	26.4
Other collection	300	$ 32	3.4	6.9	36.8	38.7	14.2
Technology and system	380	$ 284	3.1	3.9	26.8	41.2	25.0
Outsourcing	225	$ 7	3.0	3.0	71.3	11.9	10.9
Other operating	281	$ 39	1.7	6.5	16.0	53.2	22.5

University of North Carolina at Chapel Hill, School of Information and Library Science, for the Institute of Museum and Library Services

Table 5.10
Total Annual Expenditures per Library, and Trend Compared to Five Years Ago, by Range of In-Person Visits: 2007

| Range of Visits (000) | Sample (n) | Expenditure $ per Library (000) | TREND (%) | | | | |
| | | | Down | | | Up | |
			>10%	0 to 10%	Flat	0 to 10%	>10%
<10	302	82.1	2.5	6.4	20.7	49.3	21.1
10 to 49	527	255.5	2.2	6.0	11.5	48.2	32.1
50 to 249	550	804.3	1.9	4.8	9.7	49.3	34.4
250 or more	269	6,296.4	2.3	4.9	9.8	41.3	41.7

University of North Carolina at Chapel Hill, School of Information and Library Science, for the Institute of Museum and Library Services

down, 10 percent the same, and 84 percent up. Also reinforcing this evidence of the upward trend in salaries and wages expenditures are the annual ALA-APA Salary Survey surveys, where the 2008 median MLS librarian salary was estimated at $53,521, up from $42,922 in 2000, an increase of 19.8 percent.[4]

The trends in collection expenditures (print, electronic, and other) tend to be about the same, although the average print collection expenditures per library tend to be the highest of the three types of collection. Outsourcing expenditures[5] per library are estimated to be $7,000, and very little change occurred over the past five years: 6 percent of libraries say expenditures are less, 71 percent of libraries report expenditures are the same, and 22 percent say they are more now. This result is validated later in this chapter, in reporting on trends in the proportion of functions that are performed by in-library staff. The results are remarkably stable for 37 functions examined. The largest trend is with systems/IT support, in which 20 percent of libraries said in-house performance is less, 57 percent the same, and 23 percent more. The 2009 ALA "Public Library Funding & Technology Access Study" confirms that libraries rely on external IT support primarily from outside vendors/contractors (27.2%), followed by county/city IT staff (14%), consortia (12.7%), and state telecommunications network staff (3.1%).[6]

The previous two recessions (early 1990s and 2000s) affected how public library expenditures were allocated. Considering per-capita expenditures in constant dollars, trends were substantially different among staff, collection, and other operating expenditures. For example, in the 1990–1994 recession the proportion of expenditures allocated to staff increased from 63 to 69 percent. Total per-capita expenditures rose by 4.5 percent in constant dollars and expenditures for staff rose by 14.4 percent, compared with substantial decreases of 13.6 percent for collections and 10.7 percent for other types of expenditures. Similarly, the staff proportion of expenditures rose to 66 percent from 64 percent during the 2000–2004 recession. Overall total operation expenditures per capita in constant dollars increased 1.8 percent, staff increased 4.3 percent, collections decreased 11.4 percent, and other expenditures increased 3.7 percent.

A 2006 ALA study of funding issues in public libraries found that service areas impacted by revenue increases were ranked as follows: materials (average of 22.5% of libraries responding), staffing (average of 16.4% of libraries responding), electronic access (average of 11.3% of libraries responding), and hours open (average of 5% of libraries responding). Libraries reported reductions in services fairly consistently regardless of the severity of the reduction. Reductions were ranked as follows: materials (average of 68.3% of libraries responding), staffing (average of 41.6% of libraries responding), hours open (average of 24.6% of libraries responding), and electronic access (average of 12.6% of libraries responding).[7]

It may be that public library staff expenditures increased because of parent organization rules regarding employment and salaries.[8] It is also noted that collection expenditures decreased substantially, even though circulation increased about 10 percent per capita during both recessions and appears to be doing so during the current recession.

A COMPARISON OF FUNCTIONS PERFORMED IN THE LIBRARY VERSUS ELSEWHERE

Public library activities and functions are often supported by parent organizations such as county governments or library systems, consortia, networks, etc., or contractors/vendors. There are two aspects to this phenomenon. One is that the public library workforce extends well beyond public libraries themselves. The second is that libraries increase performance by utilizing outside resources to perform several functions. The extent to which work is done elsewhere is addressed by the 2007 Library Survey, in which libraries were asked about 37 functions performed in their libraries: whether they currently perform a function in their library and, if so, what proportion of the function is performed by in-library staff, and the trend in the proportion of the function performed by in-library staff (in 2007) compared to five years ago (i.e., less, same, more). The proportion performed by staff is categorized by none (zero), 1–49 percent, 50–99 percent, and 100 percent. The functions are categorized by operations/technical services (15 functions), user services (14 functions), and support services (8 functions). This information provides an indication of how much work is being done by the parent organization, library consortia, etc., or contractors. The 2007 Library Survey also obtained information about the extent to which these outside entities are used, and the ALA provides useful survey information about library networks, cooperatives, and consortia.[9]

INVOLVEMENT IN LIBRARY NETWORKS, COOPERATIVES, CONSORTIA, ETC., AND FUNCTIONS/ACTIVITIES PERFORMED BY CONTRACTOR OR VENDOR STAFF

Public (and other types of libraries) are somewhat unique in their generous cooperation through library networks, consortia, cooperatives, etc. Most public libraries (76%) reported they participate in such cooperative arrangements as a member or by providing network resources. They reported an average of 3.4 such arrangements per library. Over one-fifth (22.5%) said they participate as a source of such arrangements by providing some technical services, user services, or other support to libraries that are being funded elsewhere, and they report an average of 3 such arrangements per library. Finally, about 16.2 percent of the public libraries reported on library activities performed outside their library facilities by contract or vendor staff for activities that are normally performed in a library (table 5.11). The libraries were asked not to include popular vendor services such as OCLC, EBSCO, Lexis-Nexis, Factiva, etc., and therefore these services are not included in the numbers above.

The ALA conducted a survey of 147 library networks, cooperatives, and consortia in 2006–2007[10] that provides results from another perspective. The survey found that these organizations served 5,189 public libraries (a total of 17,126 libraries, including academic, special, and school libraries). The purposes/services provided by 75 percent or more of these organizations include communication among member libraries (directories, e-mail lists, newsletters, other publications), resource sharing, general professional development, continuing education or staff training, etc.

Table 5.11
Proportion (%) of Libraries That Participate in Cooperative Services as a Member and as a Source and Whether Any Activities Are Performed by Contract or Vendor Staff, and Average Number for Each: 2007 (n = 2,749)

	TYPE OF CONSORTIUM/NETWORK		
	Member	Source	Use of Contractor/Vendor
Proportion (%) of libraries	76.0	22.5	16.2
Average number of arrangements	3.2	3.4	3.0

University of North Carolina at Chapel Hill, School of Information and Library Science, for the Institute of Museum and Library Services

The average expenditures per organization are $2,083,719 broken down by salaries and wages ($505,179), employee benefits ($155,975), procurement of products and services ($921,605), administrative support ($138,987), and other operating expenditures ($316,177), which is somewhat different than a typical public library, in which about two-thirds of expenses are for salaries and wages. The average staff size is about 8 to 10 staff, who should be considered part of the library workforce. The ALA study's findings on the top-ranked (mean) services needed in the next 2 to 3 years are presented in figure 5.1.

PUBLIC LIBRARY RELIANCE ON NON-LIBRARY STAFF OF PARENT OR FUNDING ORGANIZATIONS

A substantial proportion of libraries rely on their parent organization for help with support functions (table 5.12). Over half of public libraries say they rely on such support for payroll processing (57.6%) and legal issues (53%). About one-third use non-library support for central IT systems maintenance (36.5%), human resource/personnel processing (32.2%), and financing (30.3%). Nearly one-fifth of libraries seek help for license and contract negotiation (19.7%). However, only 11.8 percent receive help in fund-raising, and 6.9 percent involve parent organizations for marketing or public relations. The extent of labor used from non-library staff of city, county, or library systems is not established, but in many respects these staff resources should be considered part of the library workforce as "on behalf of" labor contributions.

Table 5.12

Proportion (%) of Libraries by Type of Activities Performed by Non-Library Staff of Their Parent Organization: 2007 (n = 1,951)

Type of Activity	Proportion (%) of Libraries
Central IT systems maintenance	36.5
Human resource/personnel processing	32.2
Payroll processing	57.6
License/contract negotiations	19.7
Legal issues	53.0
Financing	30.3
Marketing/public relations	6.9
Fund-raising	11.8

University of North Carolina at Chapel Hill, School of Information and Library Science, for the Institute of Museum and Library Services

TREND IN FUNCTIONS PERFORMED BY IN-LIBRARY STAFF

As mentioned above, the functions performed in libraries are categorized by operations and technical services (15 functions), user services (14 functions), and support services (8 functions). Libraries report whether each function is currently performed

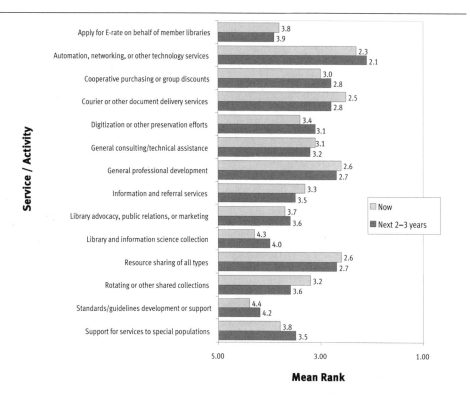

Mean Rank

American Library Association, "Library Cooperatives," www.ala.org/ala/research/librarystats/cooperatives/

Figure 5.1

Library Cooperatives' Service or Activity Priorities: Now and Over the Next Two to Three Years

(at all), the proportion (%) performed by in-library staff (0, 1–49, 50–99, and 100%), and the trend in the proportion performed by in-library staff compared to five years ago.

Tables 5.13 through 5.15 identify (1) functions for which less than 50 percent of the function is performed by in-library staff by over 50 percent of libraries, (2) functions that are performed entirely (100%) by in-library staff by 75 percent or more libraries, and (3) the trend in the level of functions performed by in-library staff as being either more or less for 10 percent or more libraries.

The results are summarized here by functions for which over 50 percent of libraries reported they perform less than 50 percent of those functions in the library. These are functions for which most libraries rely on outside sources. For example, 45.6 percent of libraries currently support cataloging (original and copy) of electronic journals, but 64 percent of the libraries do none of the function, and 2.4 percent of libraries do between 1 and 49 percent by in-library staff (see table 5.13). Six of the seven functions for which over 50 percent of libraries perform less than 50 percent of the functions in the library are electronic-related.

Secondly, libraries that perform 100 percent of the functions by library staff are observed in the survey. If 75 percent or more libraries perform 100 percent of the functions in the library, the function is noted. These are functions in which few libraries rely on outside sources. For example, 96 percent of libraries say the physical processing of journals and periodicals is currently performed by the libraries, and 89.5 percent of the libraries have all (100%) physical processing done by in-library staff (see table 5.14).

Table 5.13

Proportion (%) of Libraries That Currently Perform Functions in Which Less Than 50 Percent
Are Performed by In-Library Staff by Over 50 Percent of Libraries: 2007 (n = 316)

Function	Proportion of Libraries (%)	PROPORTION PERFORMED BY STAFF (%)			
		0	1 to 49	50 to 99	100
Cataloging (original and copy): Books—electronic	60.4	46.7	4.7	5.3	43.3
Cataloging (original and copy): Journals—electronic	45.6	64.0	2.4	1.6	32.0
Preservation: electronic	20.1	50.5	3.9	7.7	37.8
Access to Library collection: E-books	72.7	46.2	13.1	5.0	35.6
Access to Library collection: E-journals	56.6	55.4	8.3	5.5	30.8
Access to Library collection: F-report collection	50.0	46.8	6.3	7.6	39.2
Access to Library collection: Images	47.2	48.4	3.1	9.4	39.1

*University of North Carolina at Chapel Hill, School of Information and Library Science, for the Institute of Museum
and Library Services*

Most of the 37 functions are highly stable in that most libraries report the proportions of the functions performed by in-library staff are the same compared to five years ago. Functions are noted when trends in the proportion of libraries performing the functions in the library change more or less by 10 percent or more of libraries. For example, 97.7 percent of the libraries currently do physical processing of books. The trend in the proportion of libraries performing this function using in-library staff is less in 16.8 percent of libraries (see table 5.15 below).

The functions for which less than 50 percent of the function is performed by in-library staff for over 50 percent of libraries are given in table 5.13. The functions that are done by less than 50 percent of in-library staff are mostly electronic-related functions and are currently done by or for fewer libraries than the print-related functions.

Many functions are performed entirely (100%) by in-library staff. The nine functions for which 75 percent of libraries perform them in-house entirely are given in table 5.14. Collection development, cataloging, and physical processing of print collections are currently done by or for most libraries and tend to be performed entirely (100%) by in-library staff in a majority of libraries (75% or more). Circulation and interlibrary lending and borrowing are currently done by or for nearly all libraries and are performed entirely in the libraries for most libraries (i.e., over 75% of them).

Management is the only support function done by or for nearly all libraries and done entirely by in-library staff. This confirms the results shown in table 5.12 which show that many public libraries depend on parent organizations or funders to perform some support functions.

The trends in proportion of functions performed by in-library staff have been remarkably stable across functions. Table 5.15 displays those functions for which

Table 5.14

Proportion (%) of Libraries That Currently Perform Functions Entirely by In-Library Staff
Reported by 75 Percent or More of Libraries: 2007 (n = 316)

Function	Proportion of Libraries (%)	PROPORTION PERFORMED BY STAFF (%)			
		0	1 to 49	50 to 99	100
Collection development: Print materials	98.7	1.2	6.0	11.3	81.5
Cataloging (original and copy): Journals—print	89.9	11.0	2.8	4.9	81.3
Cataloging (original and copy): Audio visual materials	96.1	4.6	4.6	12.8	77.9
Physical processing: Journals/ periodicals	96.0	4.1	2.0	4.4	89.5
Physical processing: Special collections	87.0	11.8	3.2	6.4	78.6
Access to Library collection: Circulation of print materials	93.3	1.2	1.0	8.0	89.8
Interlibrary loan/document delivery: Lending	98.1	3.3	5.3	8.7	82.6
Interlibrary loan/document delivery: Borrowing	99.3	2.1	4.9	10.1	82.8
Management	99.3	0.6	3.8	9.6	86.0

University of North Carolina at Chapel Hill, School of Information and Library Science, for the Institute of Museum and Library Services

Table 5.15

Proportion (%) of Libraries That Currently Perform Functions and Proportion of the Functions
Performed by In-Library Staff Compared to Five Years Ago: 2007 (n = 316)

Function	Current (%)	TREND IN PROPORTION (%)		
		Less	Same	More
Collection development: Electronic materials	83.9	8.6	79.4	12.0*
Cataloging (original and copy): Books—print	96.2	12.8*	80.7	6.6
Physical processing: Books	97.7	16.8*	76.9	6.3
Access to library collection: E-books	72.7	2.6	78.9	18.4*
Reference and research: Database search by staff	97.9	12.0*	79.5	8.5
Reference and research: User orientation and training	95.8	3.5	89.5	11.9*
Systems, IT support	92.5	20.4*	57.2	22.4*
Web content management	90.2	8.4	70.1	21.6*

* Denotes change of plus or minus 10 percent from five years ago

University of North Carolina at Chapel Hill, School of Information and Library Science, for the Institute of Museum and Library Services

the trend in functions performed by in-library staff has changed more or less than 10 percent compared to five years ago. These changes are noted with an asterisk.

The functions in which the trend (compared to five years ago) is less for 10 percent or more libraries are cataloging (original and copy) of print books (12.8%), physical processing of books (16.8%), reference and research, including database searches by staff (12%), and systems and IT support (20.4%), which has about an equal positive trend (22.4%). Other functions with a trend of 10 percent or more in-library involvement are collection development of electronic materials (12%); access to library collections (18.4%), which is consistent with the increase in collection development; reference and research that involve user orientation and training (11.9%); and web content management (21.6%). The trend in more in-library involvement may be possibly due to increases in revenue (and expenditures) over the same five-year period.

IMPORTANCE OF PUBLIC LIBRARIAN COMPETENCIES

Competencies are generally expressed as knowledge, skills, and attitudes or abilities (KSA). The competencies included in the 2007 Library Survey were taken from the literature and from experience of studies performed by the authors. The competencies are grouped by operations or technical services, user services, technology and systems, digital library management, management or administration, and general professional competencies.

Each library was asked (1) whether the competency is currently applicable to the library, (2) to rate the importance of the competency on a scale of 1 = not at all important to 5 = absolutely essential, and (3) the trend in importance compared to five years ago. The results for each competency are given below.

Operations or technical services competencies are described in table 5.16 by whether the competency is applicable, the proportion in which the competency is rated as very important or absolutely essential, the average rating, and the trend in importance. The highest-rated operations or technical services competencies are the ability to select and evaluate materials and a knowledge of sources of materials. Their average ratings of importance range from 4.21 to 3.84, with the proportion of libraries indicating that the competencies are presently very important or absolutely essential ranging from 89.1 to 74.9 percent. The trend in knowledge of sources of electronic materials is particularly high, with 81.5 percent of relevant libraries indicating its importance is somewhat to much more important now than five years ago. The proportion of libraries indicating the competencies are presently very important or absolutely essential range from 32.1 percent to 89.1 percent. The trend in importance of knowledge of sources of other materials is particularly positive (81.5% of libraries indicate it is more important now compared to five years ago).

User services competencies are given in table 5.17. The three highest-rated user services competencies are knowledge/skills to perform online database searches (4.19 average rating), knowledge of user needs and requirements (4.16 average), and knowledge of circulation principles (4.14 average). The trend in importance is generally greater now compared to five years ago for all user services competencies.

Table 5.18 examines technology or systems-related competencies. These competencies include knowledge of computer operating systems, workstations and systems, network options, and knowledge/skills to develop websites. Many of the

Table 5.16

Proportion (%) of Libraries That Indicate Operations or Technical Services Competency Is (1) Currently Applicable to Library, (2) Important or Absolutely Essential; and Average Rating of Importance and Trend in Importance Compared to Five Years Ago: 2007 (n = 395)

Librarian Competency	Proportion (%) Indicating That the Competency Is Currently Applicable to the Library	Proportion (%) Indicating That the Competency Is Presently Very Important or Absolutely Essential	Average Rating of Importance of the Competency (5-point scale, 1 = not at all important to 5 = absolutely essential)	TREND IN IMPORTANCE (%)		
				Less	Same	More
Knowledge of sources of print materials	96.1	89.1	4.19	2.9	66.2	30.9
Knowledge of sources of electronic materials	96.0	75.1	3.84	12.8	69.3	17.9
Knowledge of sources of other materials	93.5	74.9	3.89	1.9	16.5	81.5
Knowledge of cataloging principles	92.1	62.0	3.52	2.8	60.1	37.1
Knowledge of physical processing principles	89.2	64.8	3.61	20.3	61.6	18.1
Knowledge of preservation principles	86.4	50.8	3.30	15.4	72.3	12.3
Knowledge of archiving of records management principles	65.0	32.1	2.79	12.5	70.0	17.5
Collection management skills	56.3	35.5	2.80	9.3	66.2	24.5
Ability to select and evaluate materials	95.8	87.8	4.21	1.3	75.1	23.6

University of North Carolina at Chapel Hill, School of Information and Library Science, for the Institute of Museum and Library Services

libraries consider knowledge of computer operating systems and workstations and systems to be very important or absolutely essential (80.7 to 86.5% of libraries). The average ratings are 4.05 and 4.12, respectively. Many libraries that indicate the competencies are currently applicable also indicate that their importance has increased over the past five years (00.7 to 69.6% of libraries indicate they are somewhat to much more important), with the exception of knowledge/skills to develop taxonomies and thesauri.

Digital library management competencies (table 5.19) are rated relatively low (2.41 to 2.93 average ratings) except for a knowledge of systems of cataloging and classification such as Encoded Archival Description (EAD), Dublin Core, Medium Access Control (MAC), and Open Archives Initiative (OAI), which has an average rating of 3.51. About two-thirds of the libraries consider this competency applicable, but only 35.1 percent of these libraries indicate that its importance is somewhat to much more important now compared to five years ago.

There are several management or administration competencies described in table 5.20. All of these competencies have average ratings above 4.00 except for license negotiation skills (3.00 average rating)[11] and knowledge of statistical and evaluation principles (3.67). Most libraries consider these competencies to be very important or essential (64.1 to 92.3% of libraries) except for license negotiation skills (40.3%). Again, over 30 percent of the libraries say that these competencies are more important now than five years ago.

Table 5.17

Proportion (%) of Libraries That Indicate User Services Competency Is (1) Currently Applicable to Library, (2) Important or Absolutely Essential; and Average Rating of Importance and Trend in Importance Compared to Five Years Ago: 2007 (n = 399)

Librarian Competency	Proportion (%) Indicating That the Competency Is Currently Applicable to the Library	Proportion (%) Indicating That the Competency Is Presently Very Important or Absolutely Essential	Average Rating of Importance of the Competency (5-point scale, 1 = not at all important to 5 = absolutely essential)	TREND IN IMPORTANCE (%)		
				Less	Same	More
Knowledge of circulation principles	98.0	83.6	4.14	1.9	78.6	19.5
Knowledge of ILL/document delivery principles	93.5	74.3	3.86	5.4	61.8	32.9
Ability to conduct appropriate reference interviews	95.2	81.6	4.04	5.7	71.0	23.2
Knowledge/skills to perform online database searches	98.0	87.0	4.19	2.5	19.4	78.1
Skills in training and bibliographic instruction in general	88.2	52.7	3.34	6.0	65.3	28.7
Knowledge/skills in training and bibliographic instruction for electronic services	87.1	68.4	3.68	2.1	30.0	67.9
Knowledge/skills with users having non-technical backgrounds	97.4	80.1	3.97	4.8	36.1	59.2
Knowledge of user needs and requirements	98.5	88.1	4.16	1.1	66.7	32.2
Technical knowledge/skills	96.4	82.3	4.04	1.1	31.2	67.7
Web content management skills	73.5	62.3	3.52	1.8	20.8	77.4

University of North Carolina at Chapel Hill, School of Information and Library Science, for the Institute of Museum and Library Services

Table 5.18
Proportion (%) of Libraries That Indicate Technology or Systems-Related Competency Is (1) Currently Applicable to Library, (2) Important or Absolutely Essential; and Average Rating of Importance and Trend in Importance Compared to Five Years Ago: 2007 (n = 388)

Librarian Competency	Proportion (%) Indicating That the Competency Is Currently Applicable to the Library	Proportion (%) Indicating That the Competency Is Presently Very Important or Absolutely Essential	Average Rating of Importance of the Competency (5-point scale, 1 = not at all important to 5 = absolutely essential)	TREND IN IMPORTANCE (%)		
				Less	Same	More
Knowledge of computer operating systems	93.2	80.7	4.05	2.3	31.6	66.1
Knowledge of workstations and systems	85.3	86.5	4.12	1.7	35.8	62.5
Knowledge of network options	80.2	63.0	3.62	20.1	37.2	60.7
Knowledge/skills to develop websites	73.7	63.0	3.55	3.3	27.1	69.6
Knowledge/skills to develop taxonomies and thesauri	28.6	22.8	2.44	12.9	66.2	20.9

University of North Carolina at Chapel Hill, School of Information and Library Science, for the Institute of Museum and Library Services

Table 5.19
Proportion (%) of Libraries That Indicate Digital Library Management Competency Is (1) Currently Applicable to Library, (2) Important or Absolutely Essential; and Average Rating of Importance and Trend in Importance Compared to Five Years Ago: 2007 (n = 368)

Librarian Competency	Proportion (%) Indicating That the Competency Is Currently Applicable to the Library	Proportion (%) Indicating That the Competency Is Presently Very Important or Absolutely Essential	Average Rating of Importance of the Competency (5-point scale, 1 = not at all important to 5 = absolutely essential)	TREND IN IMPORTANCE (%)		
				Less	Same	More
Knowledge of markup languages (e.g., HTML, XML, SGML, TEL)	45.2	31.4	2.77	12.0	41.4	46.6
Design skills (e.g., interface, graphic)	48.2	37.3	2.93	3.5	39.9	56.6
Data transformation skills (e.g., XSLT)	21.0	24.5	2.43	8.3	57.0	34.7
Programming languages (e.g., ASP, PHP, Java, C++)	21.6	22.6	2.41	6.9	55.4	37.7
Database management skills (e.g., SQL, MySQL, Access)	42.8	37.9	2.91	5.5	43.4	51.1
Systems of cataloging and classification (e.g., EAD, Dublin Core, MAC, OAI)	68.1	58.8	3.51	5.3	59.6	35.1

University of North Carolina at Chapel Hill, School of Information and Library Science, for the Institute of Museum and Library Services

Table 5.20

Proportion (%) of Libraries That Indicate Management or Administration Competency Is (1) Currently Applicable to Library, (2) Important or Absolutely Essential; and Average Rating of Importance and Trend in Importance Compared to Five Years Ago: 2007 (n = 381)

Librarian Competency	Proportion (%) Indicating That the Competency Is Currently Applicable to the Library	Proportion (%) Indicating That the Competency Is Presently Very Important or Absolutely Essential	Average Rating of Importance of the Competency (5-point scale, 1 = not at all important to 5 = absolutely essential)	TREND IN IMPORTANCE (%)		
				Less	Same	More
Management knowledge and skills	97.2	89.5	4.35	1.1	66.1	32.8
License negotiation skills	42.7	40.3	3.00	4.6	57.9	37.6
Knowledge of planning and budgeting principles	95.4	91.1	4.41	0.6	64.1	35.3
Knowledge of statistical and evaluation principles	89.0	64.1	3.67	1.2	64.9	33.9
Skills to develop library policies	96.2	80.8	4.02	0.8	69.4	29.8
Skills to recruit, interview, and hire personnel	93.3	80.7	4.08	0.9	67.0	32.2
Knowledge of legal, financial, and funding issues	90.7	79.3	4.05	0.9	55.9	43.2
Public relations/marketing skills	97.1	85.7	4.12	0.6	44.9	54.6
Leadership skills	98.2	92.3	4.31	0.3	62.3	37.4
Knowledge of funders' expectations of the library	93.0	83.3	4.10	1.8	55.5	42.7

University of North Carolina at Chapel Hill, School of Information and Library Science, for the Institute of Museum and Library Services

Table 5.21 presents eight general professional librarian competencies. All but knowledge of subject specialties and foreign languages (2.88 and 2.53 average ratings) are rated highly. The highest rating is positive attitude toward users and colleagues (4.57 average rating of importance). Various communication skills are all rated highly (3.90 to 4.43). The two lowest-rated competencies are (1) knowledge of foreign languages (2.53), with only 41.5 percent of libraries saying it is currently applicable to their library, although the trend in importance is up (41.4% of libraries); and (2) knowledge of subject specialties such as science, law, engineering, etc. (2.91), which again is currently applicable to only 55.2 percent of libraries, and with the trend being up in only 12.4 percent of libraries.

Table 5.21

Proportion (%) of Libraries That Indicate General Professional Competency Is (1) Currently Applicable to Library, (2) Important or Absolutely Essential; and Average Rating of Importance and Trend in Importance Compared to Five Years Ago: 2007 (n = 383)

Librarian Competency	Proportion (%) Indicating That the Competency Is Currently Applicable to the Library	Proportion (%) Indicating That the Competency Is Presently Very Important or Absolutely Essential	Average Rating of Importance of the Competency (5-point scale, 1 = not at all important to 5 = absolutely essential)	TREND IN IMPORTANCE (%)		
				Less	Same	More
Communicate effectively in writing	99.2	90.3	4.31	0.8	74.0	25.1
Communicate effectively orally	100.0	94.8	4.43	0.3	73.6	26.1
Make presentations to groups	96.6	76.9	3.90	2.3	64.8	33.0
Critical thinking skills for library problems	99.7	89.8	4.38	—	63.5	36.5
Positive attitudes toward users and colleagues	100.0	95.6	4.57	0.3	71.7	28.0
Knowledge of subject specialties (e.g., science, law, engineering, etc.)	55.2	29.0	2.91	6.4	81.3	12.4
Knowledge of foreign languages	41.5	21.9	2.53	2.6	55.9	41.4
Knowledge of behavior management skills (i.e., dealing with difficult patrons)	97.4	84.5	4.10	1.4	62.1	36.5

University of North Carolina at Chapel Hill, School of Information and Library Science, for the Institute of Museum and Library Services

PUBLIC LIBRARY SUPPORT OF EDUCATION AND TRAINING

The 2007 Library Survey provides an indication of the proportion of public libraries that support various types of education or training and the average expenditures per library for each type. It also shows the trend in whether the libraries are spending less, the same, or more now than five years ago.

Most public libraries provide support for attendance at professional meetings: this is supported by an average of $2,410 per library, with 33.5 percent spending more now than five years ago. Thirty-eight percent of libraries support formal education through evening classes, 72 percent through virtual university courses, and about 35 percent through certificate for advancement. The total average expenditure per library for this formal education support is $1,750. Some of the libraries are spending more for these means of education (22%, 25%, and 10% for evening classes, virtual courses, and certificates, respectively). Other types of training include external workshops provided by nearly all libraries (99%), with $1,530 average expenditure; and internal formal training (79% of libraries), with $1,380 average expenditure. Both have trends for more expenditure (32% and 30%, respectively). The proportion of librarians who attend these education and training events is discussed in chapter 6.

Notes

1. 2010 Harris Poll Quorum Household Survey, www.ala.org/ala/research/librarystatspublic/2010HarrisPoll.pdf.

2. American Library Association, "A Perfect Storm Brewing: Budget Cuts Threaten Public Library Services at a Time of Increased Demand," 2010, www.ala.org/ala/research/initiatives/plftas/issuesbriefs/issuebrief_perfectstorm.pdf.

3. Respondents were instructed as follows: "Please consider inflation when comparing current expenditures with those from five years ago." However, this is somewhat problematic, since many librarians who report may not know the extent of inflation.

4. American Library Association, "ALA-APA Salary Survey: Librarian—Public and Academic," available at www.ala-apa.org.

5. Outsourcing includes purchases from consortia, vendors, and contractors. Some purchases are for performing a function such as cataloging or group purchases of journals.

6. American Library Association, "Libraries Connect Communities: Public Library Funding & Technology Access Study 2009–2010," 2010, available at www.ala.org/ala/research/initiatives/plftas/2009_2010/index.cfm#final report.

7. Denise M. Davis, "Funding Issues in U.S. Public Libraries, Fiscal Years 2003–2006," 2006, available at www.ala.org/ala/research/librarystats/public/fundingissuesinuspls.pdf.

8. The ALA tracks collective bargaining activities. See http://ala-apa.org/?s=collective+bargaining/.

9. American Library Association, "Library Cooperatives," www.ala.org/ala/research/librarystats/cooperatives/index.cfm.

10. Denise M. Davis, "Library Networks, Cooperatives and Consortia: A National Survey," American Library Association, 2007, available at www.ala.org/ala/research/librarystats/cooperatives/lncc/Final%20report.pdf.

11. Note that both parent or funding organizations (table 5.12) and consortia (see note 10) support license negotiations.

STATUS OF PUBLIC MLS LIBRARIANS

Chapters 2 through 5 dealt largely with public libraries. The remaining chapters (6 through 8) discuss various aspects of public librarians based on the 2007 workforce surveys of public libraries and library staff. Chapter 9 gives examples of the impact of past recessions on public librarians and libraries and some evidence on the current recession. The IMLS-sponsored workforce study was focused on librarians who have a graduate degree (typically an MLS or variant such as MA, MLIS, MSIS, etc.) from an LIS (library and information science) or similar program accredited by the American Library Association, and these librarians are also emphasized in this chapter. For the remainder of the book, these librarians are referred to as *MLS librarians* to distinguish them from professional librarians with degrees from other programs and other professionals working in a librarian capacity. This chapter presents past trends in library staff structure, including growth in the number of MLS librarians, other professionals working in a librarian capacity, other professionals working in another capacity, paraprofessionals, and non-professionals. However, the emphasis is placed on MLS librarians in terms of their work areas or departments, level of employment, salaries, and fringe benefits. A conclusion is presented on the trends in these MLS librarian aspects and what might be expected concerning MLS librarian employment and staff structure during the current recession.

The workforce 2007 Library Survey was conducted through a web-based survey of 7,715 public libraries, of which 3,127 libraries responded. About 2,423 of these responses included staffing structure questions. Some of the 3,127 responding libraries (692) were asked to forward the web-based survey to staff, and 1,020 of the 3,892 staff respondents were MLS librarians. Note that the survey of MLS librarians is not random and some responses can be biased, although the demographics appear to be in line with other surveys. Other results are provided by the ALA and NCES/IMLS data. Trends are given by years 2002 and 2007 in order to provide common comparisons for the workforce surveys and the NCES and IMLS data.

STAFF STRUCTURE

The trend in library staffing structure is important to know because it indicates possible shifts in structure that might affect the growth in the number of MLS librarians. An indicator of changing staff structure is provided by the NCES/IMLS in 2002 and 2007 (table 6.1). The results show that the staff structure has not changed much over the five years. However, the trend varies by type of staff. Net increases from 2002 to 2007 were: MLS librarians (+5.7%), other librarians (+3.4%), and other staff (+6.8%). The total FTE library staff increased by 6.2 percent during this period.

Another source of evidence is provided by an ALA report, "Diversity Counts," by D. M. Davis and T. D. Hall, in which a table shows the number of MLS and other librarians annually from 1989 to 2004. The number and proportion of MLS librarians is presented in five-year increments in table 6.2. In 1989 the proportion of librarians that were MLS librarians was less (61.9%) but was relatively consistent in the other years, which is similar to the 2002 to 2007 period (67.7% and 68.2%, respectively).

Public library staff are categorized as MLS librarians, other professionals (i.e., with a relevant degree) working in a librarian capacity, other professionals working in another capacity (e.g., administration, systems specialist, etc.), paraprofessional staff, non-professional staff, and unpaid staff/volunteers. The 2007 Library Survey provides an estimate in 2002 and 2007 of the proportion of public libraries having such staff and the average number of each type of staff per library. The staffing structure is examined for each of the two years in terms of the proportion of paid staff by ranges of the number of annual in-person visits (as a proxy measure for the size of the library).

The numbers of staff in various categories are given as head counts; that is, the number of employees regardless of whether they are full-time or part-time. National surveys (NCES/IMLS) report full-time equivalents (FTEs), which are always lower than head counts, if there are part-time employees. The head count is used because it forms the basis for projecting data from the Staff Survey in which samples are of

Table 6.1
Number and Proportion (%) of MLS Librarians, Other Librarians, and Other Staff (FTE)
in 2002 and 2007

Category of Staff	2002		2007	
	Number	(%)	Number	(%)
MLS librarians	30,428	22.3	32,173	22.2
Other librarians	14,492	10.6	14,980	10.4
Other staff	91,299	67.0	97,500	67.4
Total	136,219	99.9	144,653	100.0

Source: NCES 2002, IMLS 2007

University of North Carolina at Chapel Hill, School of Information and Library Science, for the Institute of Museum and Library Services

Table 6.2

Number of MLS Librarians and Other Librarians (FTE) with an MLS and Proportion (%) of MLS Librarians in 1989, 1994, 1999, and 2004

| | MLS LIBRARIANS | | OTHER LIBRARIANS | | |
Year	Number	(%)	Number	(%)	Total
1989	20,523	61.9	12,645	38.1	33,168
1994	25,879	68.0	12,169	32.0	38,048
1999	28,822	69.0	12,950	31.0	41,772
2004	30,560	67.9	14,477	32.1	45,037

Source: D. M. Davis and T. D. Hall, "Diversity Counts"

University of North Carolina at Chapel Hill, School of Information and Library Science, for the Institute of Museum and Library Services

staff regardless of full-time or part-time status. Some data given below are NCES/IMLS-reported FTE counts for comparison.

Table 6.3 provides estimates of the proportion of libraries that employ the staff and the average number of staff per library by category of library staff in 2002 and 2007. The 2007 results are from the 2007 Library Survey, and the 2002 estimates are based on reported approximate numbers for five years earlier.[1] About two-thirds of public libraries (63.2%) reported an MLS librarian on the staff in 2007. All public libraries average about 2.1 such librarians per library (head count), or 3.3 in libraries with MLS librarians. Nearly the same proportion of libraries (58.4%) reported employing other professionals working in a librarian and/or other capacity, with an average of 0.9 such professional staff per library.

The five-year trend in the proportion of libraries having various types of staff was a 3 to 6 percent increase except for other professionals working in another capacity: 21.3 percent more libraries indicated they employed such staff, and the average number per library increased 13.7 percent. The trend in average size of the staff was highest for paraprofessionals (16.7%) and least for other professionals working in a librarian capacity (2.9%), which is consistent with observations given earlier. The average number of MLS librarians increased by 9.4 percent over that period of time (see chapter 8). The NCES and IMLS report an increase of 5.7 percent of FTE MLS librarians in 2007 (32,173) from 2002 (30,428).

Table 6.4 describes the survey estimates of the total number of each type of paid staff in 2002 and 2007 and the proportion of total paid staff represented by each type. Again, the numbers of staff are reported as head counts. For example, there were estimated to be 36,169 MLS librarians in 2007, while the IMLS reported 32,173 FTE MLS librarians in 2007. The method used to estimate head count from FTE is presented in chapter 8. MLS librarians represented about 20 percent of total paid staff in both 2002 (164,739 total staff) and 2007 (181,622 total staff). The NCES/IMLS report that FTE MLS librarians represented just over 22 percent of total FTE staff. Generally, there appears to be little difference in the structure of staff between 2002 and 2007 reported by the NCES and IMLS.

The staff structure is further examined by ranges in the number of visits to the library (<10,000; 10,000 to 49,999; 50,000 to 249,999; 250,000 or more) as a proxy for the size of the library, based on the 2007 Library Survey. There seems to be little

Table 6.3
Proportion (%) of Libraries and Average Number (Head Count) per Library of Library
Staff, Staff Category: 2002 and 2007

Category of Staff	Sample (n)	2002 (%)	2002 Average	2007 (%)	2007 Average	5-Year Proportion (%) of Change in: (%)	5-Year Proportion (%) of Change in: Average
Librarian with graduate degree from accredited program	2,423	61.1	1.943	63.2	2.125	3.4	9.4
Other professional working in librarian capacity	2,424	35.9	0.545	37.9	0.561	5.6	2.9
Other professional working in another capacity	2,424	16.9	0.329	20.5	0.374	21.3	13.7
Paraprofessional	2,425	75.8	2.831	79.9	3.305	5.4	16.7
Non-professional	2,422	63.0	4.030	65.6	4.305	4.1	6.8
Total paid staff	—	—	9.678	—	10.670	—	10.3
Unpaid staff/volunteer	2,415	49.8	4.380	55.9	6.430	12.2	46.8

University of North Carolina at Chapel Hill, School of Information and Library Science, for the Institute of Museum and Library Services

Table 6.4
Proportion (%) and Total Number of Paid Staff (Head Count), by Staff Category:
2002 and 2007 (n = 2,423)

Category of Staff	2002 (%)	2002 Total	2007 (%)	2007 Total
Librarian with graduate degree from accredited program	20.1	33,074	19.9	36,169
Other professional working in librarian capacity	5.6	9,277	5.3	9,549
Other professional working in another capacity	3.4	5,600	3.5	6,366
Paraprofessional	29.3	48,189	31.0	56,258
Non-professional	41.6	68,599	40.3	73,280
Total	100.0	164,739	100.0	181,622

University of North Carolina at Chapel Hill, School of Information and Library Science, for the Institute of Museum and Library Services

difference in the structure of staff between 2002 and 2007 for each range of in-person visits (i.e., the proportions do not change much in 2007 from 2002). However, the structure itself varies somewhat among the ranges of visits. For example, the proportion of staff represented by MLS librarians increases by number of visits (i.e., about 10% for less than 10,000 visits up to about 24% for those with more than 250,000 visits). Generally, professionals working in a librarian capacity and paraprofessional representation appear to decline with the number of visits, whereas non-professionals increase.

We compared trends in the average number of professionals per library, including MLS librarians, other professionals working in a librarian capacity, and in another capacity by range of visits. The proportion of libraries with fewer than 10,000 visits having MLS librarians did not change in 2007 from 2002 (about 21% of libraries), although the average number of MLS librarians per small library declined from 0.31 to 0.25 per library (about a 19.4% decrease). However, as the size of libraries increased, the trend in the average number of MLS librarians increased substantially. For example, libraries with 250,000 or more visits increased from 13.7 to 16.3 MLS librarians per library (a 19% increase). It appears that MLS librarians who work in small libraries were being replaced by other professionals working in a librarian capacity. The proportion of libraries having these professionals increased from 35.4 percent to 42.8 percent, and the average number per library increased from 0.44 to 0.51 professionals per library or an increase of 0.07, while the decrease in MLS librarians was 0.06.

The number of professionals working in a librarian capacity in large libraries is very small compared with the number of MLS librarians. For example, in 2007 there was an average of about 2 of these professionals compared with 16 MLS librarians in libraries with 250,000 or more visits.

In small libraries (fewer than 10,000 visits) the number of professionals working in another capacity (e.g., administration, systems, etc.) was somewhat less than those working in a librarian capacity (0.17 vs. 0.51) but much more in the largest libraries (2.96 vs. 1.94 per library).

The trend in the proportion of libraries having other professionals working in a librarian capacity decreased from about 21 percent of the smallest libraries to 6 percent of the largest ones. With professionals working in another capacity the trend in the proportion of libraries employing them did not vary much by size of libraries (about 6% of libraries), and the trend in average number increased in the ranges of about 33 percent to 48 percent. Clearly, these other professionals are increasing in importance in public libraries, due in large part to the use of computer systems, the Internet, and websites. Note that over 20 percent of libraries indicated more systems/IT support and web content management being performed in the library (see table 5.15).

We observed the trends in all professional staff, as well as non-professional staff, by range in the number of visits in 2007 from 2002. For libraries having fewer than 10,000 visits, the proportion of libraries employing professional staff increased to 55.7 percent in 2007 from 51.9 percent in 2002, and the average number of professionals per library increased to 1.03 from 0.94 (a 9.6% increase). However, the average number of professionals per library in large libraries (over 250,000 visits) increased by 25.7 percent from 2002 to 2007. The increase in the number of non-professionals was less than for professionals in both size categories. For libraries with fewer than 10,000 visits, the number of non-professionals increased from 0.76 per library to 0.79 (a 3.9% increase compared with 9.6% for professionals). At large libraries (250,000 or more visits) the increase from 2002 to 2007 per library was 13.9 percent for non-professionals versus 25.7 percent for professionals. Thus, the staff structure appears to trend toward professional staff increases.

CURRENT NUMBER OF VACANCIES

Table 6.5 gives estimates of the current number of vacancies for three categories of professionals and paraprofessionals. MLS librarians represent the highest proportion of libraries that have vacancies (8.8%) and total number of vacancies (1,408

Table 6.5

Proportion (%) of Libraries Currently with Vacancies by Staff Category, Average per Library and Total Number of Vacancies per Library: 2007

Category of Staff	Sample (n)	Proportion (%) with Vacancies	Average Number of Vacancies	Total Number of Vacancies
Librarian with graduate degree from accredited program	1,816	8.8	0.081	1,408
Other professional working in librarian capacity	1,815	3.2	0.013	231
Other professional working in another capacity	1,815	3.2	0.020	333
Paraprofessional	1,816	6.7	0.044	744

University of North Carolina at Chapel Hill, School of Information and Library Science, for the Institute of Museum and Library Services

librarians). It is not clear how library respondents interpreted the number of MLS librarians in 2007, but if it was not positions as opposed to those actually currently working, the number of vacancies is comparatively high; that is, 37,578 (1,408 + 36,170) positions of which 3.9 percent are vacant. This means that the market for MLS librarians was favorable for new graduates in 2007, since there were a large number of vacancies (see also chapters 7 and 8).

TYPE OF WORK DONE BY MLS LIBRARIANS AND THEIR LEVEL OF EMPLOYMENT

The 2007 Staff Survey asked MLS librarians if their library was organized by departments, and if so, in which department (or area) they primarily work (i.e., spend most of their time). Table 6.6 gives the proportion of MLS librarians who work in each area and the total number of MLS librarians who work in those areas (note that values in tables 6.6 and 6.7 are rounded to the nearest ten). Some MLS librarians (6.8%) work in public libraries that are not organized by department. Most MLS librarians (54.7%) work in user-related services such as user/community services (including circulation, interlibrary loan, document delivery, children's and youth services, adult services, etc.) and reference and research (including training, bibliographic instruction, technology instruction, research, and information and referral). About one of eight MLS librarians work in administration (not specific to a particular department).

MLS librarians were also asked to report their current level of employment, as shown in table 6.7. Over half (54.5%) of MLS librarians work in some kind of supervisory or administrative capacity while 40.4 percent work in a non-supervising capacity. This has some bearing on LIS education because more than half the public MLS librarian workforce have management and administrative responsibilities, requiring some education or training to perform this work (see chapter 7 on career paths of public MLS librarians).

Table 6.6

Proportion (%) and Total Number of MLS Librarians, by Areas/Departments Where They Primarily Work: 2007 (n = 803)

Work Areas/Departments	MLS Librarians	
	%	Total
Not organized by department	6.8	2,460
Administration	12.5	4,520
Acquisitions	1.5	540
Technical services	6.2	2,240
User/community services	22.8	8,250
Reference and research	31.9	11,540
Special collections	0.7	250
Systems	1.6	580
Other	16.0	5,790
Total	100.0	36,170

University of North Carolina at Chapel Hill, School of Information and Library Science, for the Institute of Museum and Library Services

Table 6.7

Proportion (%) and Total Number of MLS Librarians, by Level of Employment in the Library: 2007 (n = 1,019)

Level of Employment	MLS Librarians	
	%	Total
Library director	6.2	2,240
Assistant or associate director	4.7	1,700
Department or branch head	31.4	11,360
Other supervising capacity	12.2	4,410
Librarian or staff in a non-supervisory capacity	40.4	14,610
Other	5.1	1,850
All	100.0	36,170

University of North Carolina at Chapel Hill, School of Information and Library Science, for the Institute of Museum and Library Services

Table 6.8

Proportion (%) of Surveyed Public MLS Librarians, by Ranges of Annual Salaries: 2007 (n = 676)

Annual Salary Range ($)	Proportion of MLS Librarians (%)
Under $30,000	11.3
$30,000 to $39,999	24.9
$40,000 to $49,999	24.4
$50,000 to $74,999	31.7
$75,000 to $99,999	6.1
$100,000 or more	1.6
Total	100.0

University of North Carolina at Chapel Hill, School of Information and Library Science, for the Institute of Museum and Library Services

SALARIES AND WAGES OF SURVEYED PUBLIC MLS LIBRARIANS

Salary ranges are given in table 6.8, and hourly wages are shown later in table 6.15.

Salary level is examined by gender, level of employment, and years of experience below. First, salary level by gender is given in table 6.9. It appears that a higher proportion of males than females make $75,000 or more annual salary (even though only 34 percent of males are over age 50 vs. 43 percent of females), and a lower proportion of males make less than $30,000.

Table 6.9
Proportion (%) of Surveyed Public MLS Librarians, by Ranges of Annual Salaries
and by Gender: 2007

Annual Salary Range ($)	PROPORTION OF MLS LIBRARIANS (%)		
	Male (n = 134)	Female (n = 633)	Total (n = 767)
Under $30,000	7.5	12.2	11.3
$30,000 to $39,999	25.4	24.8	24.9
$40,000 to $49,999	20.1	25.3	24.4
$50,000 to $74,999	32.8	31.4	31.7
$75,000 to $99,999	11.2	5.0	6.1
$100,000 or more	3.0	1.3	1.6
Total	100.0	100.0	100.0

University of North Carolina at Chapel Hill, School of Information and Library Science, for the Institute of Museum and Library Services

Table 6.10
Proportion (%) of Surveyed Public MLS Librarians, by Ranges of Annual Salaries and Primary
Level of Employment in the Library: 2007

Annual Salary Range ($)	PRIMARY LEVEL OF EMPLOYMENT (%)				
	Library Director (n = 59)	Assistant or Associate Director (n = 45)	Department or Branch Head (n = 278)	Other Supervisory (n = 95)	Non-Supervisory (n = 258)
Under $30,000	3.4	6.7	10.4	11.6	15.9
$30,000 to $39,999	8.5	8.9	16.5	22.1	42.6
$40,000 to $49,999	11.9	8.9	29.5	20.0	26.4
$50,000 to $74,999	39.0	53.3	37.4	41.1	14.7
$75,000 to $99,999	28.8	15.6	5.4	4.2	0.4
$100,000 or more	8.5	6.7	0.7	1.1	—
Total	100.1	100.1	99.9	100.1	100.0

Sums may exceed 100 percent due to rounding.

University of North Carolina at Chapel Hill, School of Information and Library Science, for the Institute of Museum and Library Services

Primary level of employment has an obvious bearing on annual salary, as shown in table 6.10.[2] The salary levels of the primary levels of employment are about what one would expect.

Annual salary based on years of employment is summarized in table 6.11. An appreciable proportion of MLS librarians with 10 or more years of experience make less than $30,000 annual salaries.

As mentioned above, there is a discrepancy in average salaries between males and females, that is, $43,500 for males and $38,900 for females. This discrepancy exists regardless of years of experience or level of employment, as shown in tables 6.12 and 6.13. It is not clear whether other factors contribute to this discrepancy in salaries between males and females.

Table 6.11

Proportion (%) of Surveyed Public MLS Librarians, by Ranges
of Annual Salaries and by Ranges of Years of Experience in a
Librarian Capacity: 2007

| | YEARS OF EXPERIENCE | | |
Annual Salary Range ($)	‹ 10 years (%) (n = 231)	10 to 19 years (%) (n = 244)	20 or more years (%) (n = 292)
Under $30,000	9.5	13.9	11.6
$30,000 to $39,999	52.4	16.0	9.6
$40,000 to $49,999	24.2	28.3	20.9
$50,000 to $74,999	12.6	38.1	41.8
$75,000 to $99,999	1.3	3.3	12.3
$100,000 or more	—	0.4	3.8
Total	100.0	100.0	100.0

*University of North Carolina at Chapel Hill, School of Information and Library Science,
for the Institute of Museum and Library Services*

Table 6.12

Average Salaries of Surveyed Public MLS Librarians,
by Gender and by Years of Experience: 2007

| | AVERAGE SALARY ($) | |
Years of Experience	Male (n = 189)	Female (n = 1,108)
Less than 10 years	$32,800	$28,500
10 to 19 years	$42,600	$34,600
20 or more years	$63,400	$49,000

*University of North Carolina at Chapel Hill, School of Information and
Library Science, for the Institute of Museum and Library Services*

Table 6.13

Average Salaries of Surveyed Public MLS Librarians,
by Gender and by Primary Level of Employment: 2007

| | AVERAGE SALARY ($) | |
Primary Level of Employment	Male (n = 224)	Female (n = 1,235)
Director	$77,000	$51,500
Assistant/associate director	$65,900	$47,100
Department/branch head	$47,400	$42,100
Other supervisory capacity	$43,500	$38,100
Non-supervisory capacity	$32,200	$26,700
Other	$43,800	$33,100

*University of North Carolina at Chapel Hill, School of Information and
Library Science, for the Institute of Museum and Library Services*

Table 6.14
Proportion (%) and Average Ratings of Satisfaction (1 = low to 5 = high)
with Salaries of Male and Female Surveyed Public MLS Librarians: 2007

Sex	Sample (n)	SATISFACTION RATING (%)					Average
		1	2	3	4	5	
Male	350	9.1	21.1	16.3	42.0	11.4	3.25
Female	2,363	10.3	22.6	13.6	42.4	11.0	3.21

University of North Carolina at Chapel Hill, School of Information and Library Science, for the Institute of Museum and Library Services

Table 6.15
Proportion (%) of Surveyed Public MLS Librarians, by Ranges
of Hourly Wages and Equivalent Annual Salaries: 2007

Hourly Wage Range ($)	Equivalent Annual Salary ($)	Proportion of MLS Librarians (%)
Under $15.00	Under $30,300	10.7
$15.00 to $19.99	$30,300 to $40,400	22.6
$20.00 to $24.99	$40,500 to $50,500	22.6
$25.00 to $29.99	$50,000 to $60,700	4.3
$30.00 and over	$60,700 and above	24.7

University of North Carolina at Chapel Hill, School of Information and Library Science, for the Institute of Museum and Library Services

Interestingly, satisfaction with salaries does not vary much between males and females, whose average ratings are 3.25 and 3.21, respectively, as shown in table 6.14. (See chapter 7 for ratings of other work-related issues.)

Hourly wages are multiplied by the average hours spent per week by full-time librarians (38.9 hours per week) times 52 weeks to approximate equivalent annual salaries rounded to the nearest $100 in table 6.15.

The determination of method of payment to MLS librarians (i.e., annual salaries or hourly wages) depends somewhat on their employment status. For example, for the surveyed MLS librarians 86.3 percent said they are full-time employees and the rest part-time. About 2 percent said they were temporary employees, the remainder being permanent. The employment status also affects fringe benefits that are received, as discussed below.

FRINGE BENEFITS OF SURVEYED PUBLIC MLS LIBRARIANS

Fringe benefits are grouped by three types: (1) benefits that have monetary value in addition to salaries or wages, (2) benefits that permit time off for which employees are paid, and (3) other types of benefits. The value-added compensation fringe benefits (i.e., those involving monetary benefits) available to surveyed MLS librarians are shown in table 6.16. The fringe benefits given in the table reflect the proportion of public MLS librarians who receive the benefits.

Table 6.16

Proportion (%) of Surveyed Public MLS Librarians Who Receive Value-Added Compensation
Fringe Benefits and Who Pays for Them: 2007 (n = 680)

Value-Added Compensation Fringe Benefits	WHO RECEIVES (%)			WHO PAYS (%)		
	Not Available	Available but Don't Take	Receive Benefit	Parent Organization— All	Parent Organization— Some	Librarian— All
Retirement or pension	5.9	11.6	82.4	15.7	75.0	9.3
Employee medical	7.2	12.8	80.0	37.8	58.8	3.4
Family medical	9.7	56.1	34.2	10.5	62.9	26.6
Life insurance	16.9	19.1	64.0	50.0	32.3	17.7
Long-term care	45.2	34.8	20.0	18.5	21.0	60.5
Membership dues	54.3	6.2	39.5	44.7	22.4	32.9
Parking or transportation to work	69.5	5.8	24.6	45.8	14.0	40.2
Bonuses	88.9	3.3	7.8	96.0	4.0	—

University of North Carolina at Chapel Hill, School of Information and Library Science, for the Institute of Museum and Library Services

One can also examine fringe benefits by what proportion of public libraries provide them regardless of type of employee (i.e., professional or non-professional). The 2007 Library Survey provided evidence as shown in tables 6.17, 6.18, and 6.19 below. Table 6.17 provides the value-added compensation fringe benefits from the public library perspective. Comparisons of the librarian perspective with that of the library reporting for all employees show that librarians are generally favored with these benefits. For example, 7.2 percent of MLS librarians say that employee medical plans are not available to them (table 6.16), while the Library Survey shows that 12.6 percent of the libraries do not provide medical to any employees and 68.3 percent of libraries provide it only to some employees (table 6.17). Furthermore, the MLS librarians say that 40.9 percent of the parent organizations pay all (vs. 37.8% reported by the libraries). Generally, the MLS librarians benefit more in who pays for the value-added compensation benefits.

Table 6.18 shows the proportion of public libraries (central and branches) that provide paid time not at work such as holidays, sick leave, jury leave, etc., and the maximum days allowed. Most libraries provide the range of these benefits, with over 90 percent allowing holidays (25% of libraries under 10 days, 74% 11 to 19 days, 0.8% 20 to 39 days), vacation (14.1% under 10 days, 24.4% 11 to 19, 58.1% 20 to 39, and 3.5% 40 or more), or jury duty (82% under 10 days, 15% 11 to 39, and 3% 60 or more). Many other libraries (75 to 90%) allow maternity or family leave (41.5% under 10 days, 13.2% 11 to 39, 4.7% 40 to 60, and 40.6% over 60), accumulated sick leave (55% 60 days or more), training or education (93.8% up to 19 days), and military leave (88.3% up to 19 days).

Table 6.19 indicates other non-monetary fringe benefits provided by public libraries. For example, public libraries provide flexible hours (63.5% of libraries), compensatory time (62.8%), formal recognition or awards (53.1%), and cell phone (27%), as well as a few providing job sharing, library-provided home computer, adoption assistance, and child care.

Table 6.17
Proportion (%) of Public Libraries That Provide Value-Added Compensation, by Type of Fringe Benefit, Level of Provision, and Who Pays: 2007

Type of Paid Fringe Benefit	Sample (n)	LEVEL OF PROVISION			WHO PAYS		
		No Employees	Some Employees	All Employees	Employer— All	Employer— Some	Employee— All
Retirement/pension (defined)	323	15.4	50.2	34.4	29.4	66.5	4.1
Retirement/pension (flexible)	229	49.3	30.9	19.8	20.0	43.0	36.9
Employee medical	327	12.6	68.3	19.1	40.9	57.2	1.9
Family medical	316	22.9	57.0	20.1	13.0	65.9	21.1
Life insurance	310	23.1	55.2	21.7	55.8	31.6	12.5
Disability insurance	304	35.8	44.4	19.8	50.5	27.2	22.3
Long-term care	277	72.2	20.9	6.9	12.7	23.8	63.6
Subsidized parking/transportation to work	267	85.9	5.9	8.1	57.3	30.6	12.2
Membership dues	310	29.0	61.3	9.7	74.5	20.0	5.5
Paid training/education	319	14.4	47.5	38.0	51.0	49.0	—
Bonuses (variable pay)	278	73.1	14.9	12.0	97.6	2.4	—
Broadbanding	236	83.5	3.4	13.0	89.3	10.7	—
Cash incentives	271	98.5	1.0	0.6	100.0	—	—
Job- or skill-based pay	256	79.1	10.8	10.2	89.8	10.2	—
Merit pay	267	61.2	17.9	20.9	96.1	3.9	—

University of North Carolina at Chapel Hill, School of Information and Library Science, for the Institute of Museum and Library Services

Table 6.18
Proportion (%) of Public Libraries That Provide Paid Time Not at Work, by Type of Such Fringe Benefit and Range of Maximum Days Allowed: 2007

Type of Paid Time Off	Sample (n)	Proportion That Provide (%)	MAXIMUM DAYS ALLOWED (%)				
			Under 10	11 to 19	20 to 39	40 to 50	60 or Over
Holidays	343	95.6	25.2	74.0	0.8	—	—
Sick leave	339	88.9	29.0	52.8	6.5	1.3	10.4
Accumulated sick leave	323	77.7	21.3	2.5	14.4	6.9	55.0
Vacation	339	91.9	14.1	24.4	58.1	2.6	0.9
Accumulated vacation	315	65.6	34.6	13.1	34.1	13.7	7.2
Training/education	311	82.7	82.3	11.5	4.4	—	1.8
Jury leave	309	94.1	82.0	12.0	3.0	—	3.0
Military leave	248	79.2	71.8	16.5	4.7	—	7.1
Maternity/family leave	279	84.1	41.5	1.9	11.3	4.7	40.6

University of North Carolina at Chapel Hill, School of Information and Library Science, for the Institute of Museum and Library Services

Table 6.19
Proportion (%) of Public Libraries That Provide Other
Non-Monetary Fringe Benefits: 2007

Type of Fringe Benefit	Sample (n)	Provided (%)
Child care	340	0.4
Adoption assistance	338	1.2
Flexible hours	337	63.5
Formal recognition/awards	337	53.1
Compensatory time	337	62.8
Library-provided home computer	337	7.9
Job sharing	331	17.0
Cell phone	340	27.0

University of North Carolina at Chapel Hill, School of Information and Library Science, for the Institute of Museum and Library Services

THE CONSEQUENCES OF RECESSIONS AND OTHER CONCLUSIONS

Evidence from the NCES, IMLS, ALA, and the 2007 Library Survey all show a steady increase in the number of MLS librarians up to 2007 and a stable staff structure (i.e., proportion of staff who are MLS librarians, etc.). The question is what one can expect during this current recession. During the past three recessions (early 1980s, early 1990s, and early 2000s) the number of MLS librarians continued to increase, although at different rates. The early 1980s recession ran from 1978 through 1982, during which the highest unemployment rate was 9.7 percent. Based on a King Research study funded by the NCES, the number of librarians (not only MLS librarians in these results) experienced a four-year increase of 3.5 percent, and the number of librarians per 10,000 total population went from 1.35 to 1.34.[3] The staff structure remained essentially the same over these four years.

The early 1990s recession ran from 1990 to 1994, with a high of 7.5 percent unemployment. Based on NCES data, the number of MLS librarians (FTE) increased 21.6 percent over this four-year period. The number of MLS librarians per 10,000 population increased from 0.88 to 1.01 (an increase of 14.8%). The staff structure changed some in that the proportion of MLS librarians increased from 19.7 percent to 22.9 percent, with a small decrease in other librarians and non-librarians.

The 2000 to 2004 recession (with a 6% highest unemployment rate) showed an increase of 3.7 percent in the number of MLS librarians (FTE), but a slight decrease in their number per 10,000 population from 1.09 to 1.07 (a decrease of 1.8%). Even though a decrease, the average actually increased from 1.01 in 1994 to 1.07 per 10,000 population in 2004. The staff structure remained consistent over those four years. See chapter 9 for details of these results.

The Library Survey of MLS librarians (2007) shows that there were about 36,169 MLS librarians (head count) employed at that time with 1,408 positions vacant, or about 3.9 percent of all available positions. About 8.8 percent of libraries had such vacancies.

The MLS librarian survey asked about the areas or departments where they primarily work, which provides an indicator of the type of work they are doing. It also observed the level of employment of the MLS librarians. Of those who provided an answer, 57.5 percent work in a supervisory or administrative capacity (i.e., director, assistant director, branch head, etc.). Thus, many are in a non-supervisory capacity. About 6.8 percent work in a library without a department, but of those who do, most (70.9%) work in user/community-related services (i.e., circulation, interlibrary loan, children's and youth services, etc.) or reference and research (i.e., information and referral, instruction, etc.).

MLS librarian salaries (MLS survey) show a wide range, from 11.3 percent of them under $30,000 to 7.7 percent at $75,000 and above. A higher proportion of female MLS librarians make under $30,000 (12.2 vs. 7.5% for males), and fewer of them make $75,000 or more (6.3 vs. 14.2%). Examined by years of experience, females make less than males at all three ranges of experience (under 10 years, 10 to 19 years, and 20 or more years), and they make less at five levels of employment. Surprisingly, females rate (1 to 5) their satisfaction with salaries only slightly less than males (3.21 vs. 3.25 average rating).

MLS librarians appear to receive good fringe benefits, including value-added compensation such as employee medical (80% receive, and only 3.4% pay all themselves), retirement or pension (82.4% receive, and 9.3% pay all themselves), and so on. Most libraries provide lenient time off (with adequate number of days off), and many provide flexible hours (63.5% of libraries) and compensatory time (62.8%). The fringe benefits received appear to help compensate for low salaries. Note that the proportion of libraries that employ various categories of staff and the average number of these staff per library are based on a common number of libraries in 2007 (central and branches), even though there were 0.7 percent fewer libraries in 2002.

Notes

1. The proportion of libraries that employ various categories of staff and the average number per library are based on a common number of libraries in 2007 (central and branches) even though there were 0.7 percent fewer libraries in 2002.

2. Sums of proportions (%) may not add up to 100 percent due to rounding.

3. M. D. Cooper, N. A. Van House, and N. K. Roderer, King Research, Inc., *Library Human Resources: A Study of Supply and Demand, 1983* (Chicago: American Library Association, 1983).

EVIDENCE OF CAREER PATHS OF PUBLIC MLS LIBRARIANS

The 2007 Staff Survey of public MLS librarians (n = 960) asked several questions that provide evidence of the career paths of these librarians. In particular, it examined their experience prior to working as professional librarians, the length of time between their receiving an MLS degree and becoming employed in public libraries, their reasons for leaving public libraries, and so on. They were also asked about how well their LIS education prepared them for their work, their attitude toward work-related issues, and whether they would choose librarianship again as a career. These aspects of career paths and attitudes toward librarianship are highly relevant to the future of the library workforce and could influence the 10-year forecast of the number of MLS librarians needed, as discussed in chapter 8.

PRIOR WORKING EXPERIENCE OF SURVEYED PUBLIC MLS LIBRARIANS

Some MLS librarians had prior experience working in a library full-time or as a professional in another capacity before joining the library workforce. For example, 38.3 percent of MLS librarians said they had previously worked in a library in a full-time capacity, but not as a librarian, and nearly as many had worked as a professional in another occupation (34.6%). The length of time working in these capacities is given in table 7.1. Those with 2 to 4 years and 5 to 9 years of full-time work experience were more likely to report having worked in a library (69.2% compared with 58.5%). For those with 10 to 14 years of full-time experience, other occupations were predominant.

Table 7.1

Proportion (%) of Surveyed Public MLS Librarians Who Had Worked Full-Time in a Library or in Another Occupation before Joining the Library Workforce, by Range of Years Worked: 2007 (n = 847)

Range of Years Worked	PROPORTION (%) OF MLS LIBRARIANS WHO WORKED IN:	
	A Library	Another Occupation
Less than 2	11.5	11.4
2 to 4	38.9	31.0
5 to 9	30.3	27.5
10 to 14	9.5	19.7
15 or more	9.8	10.4
Total	100.0	100.0

University of North Carolina at Chapel Hill, School of Information and Library Science, for the Institute of Museum and Library Services

Current MLS librarians who worked previously full-time in a library appear to have spent somewhat less time doing so than those who worked in another occupation. This suggests that their previous library experience may have enticed them to seek a graduate library degree.

EDUCATION PATTERNS, INITIAL HIRING, AND MLS LIBRARIAN OPINION OF THEIR LIS EDUCATION

Many surveyed MLS librarians not only had extensive work experience prior to entering the library workforce, but they also had different levels of education background as demonstrated by their other degrees earned (table 7.2).

A remarkable finding is that 28.6 percent of public MLS librarians were 35 years and older when they received their MLS degree, which also relates to their prior work experience (table 7.3).

Other aspects of careers are examined by years of experience as an MLS librarian; that is, less than 10 years, 10 to 19 years, and 20 or more years. Some librarians are not employed right after they receive their degree (MLS or PhD), as shown in table 7.4.

Table 7.2

Proportion (%) of Surveyed Public MLS Librarians, by Degree Earned: 2007 (n = 944)

Degree Earned	Proportion of MLS Librarians (%)
PhD or equivalent	1.5
MS, MA, or equivalent	15.0
BS, BA, or equivalent	72.1
LMS certification (first)	6.9

University of North Carolina at Chapel Hill, School of Information and Library Science, for the Institute of Museum and Library Services

Table 7.3

Proportion (%) of Surveyed Public MLS Librarians, by Age at Which They Earned MLS Degree: 2007 (n = 944)

Age Category (Years)	Proportion of MLS Librarians (%)
Under 25	27.3
25 to 29	27.7
30 to 34	16.4
35 and over	28.6

University of North Carolina at Chapel Hill, School of Information and Library Science, for the Institute of Museum and Library Services

Table 7.4

Proportion (%) of Surveyed Public MLS Librarians, by the Number of Years First Employed after Receiving Degree and by Ranges of Years of Experience: 2007 (n = 938)

Years First Employed after Receiving Degree	All MLS Librarians	‹10 years (%)	10 to 19 years (%)	20 or more years (%)
First year	74.6	74.8	71.7	76.7
One year later	18.7	17.9	21.5	16.9
Two years later	3.2	3.7	4.2	1.8
3 to 5 years later	2.0	1.7	1.3	3.3
Over 5 years later	1.4	2.0	1.3	1.2
Total	99.9	100.1	100.0	99.9

Sums may exceed 100 percent due to rounding.

University of North Carolina at Chapel Hill, School of Information and Library Science, for the Institute of Museum and Library Services

About three-fourths of the current MLS librarians were employed in the same year they received their degree, and about 93 percent were employed within one year later. It is also estimated that about 1,260 librarians who graduated in 2007 were employed in public libraries.

The proportion of librarians who are employed within one year of graduation is nearly the same regardless of the three ranges of years of experience. This suggests that the public library labor market has been consistent in employing new graduates. However, the survey is only of those librarians who are currently employed in public libraries. Some who left the public library workforce might have had different initial hiring experiences. The remaining graduates who were employed in libraries later than the first year after graduation may have had limitations to initial employment due to further education, geographic location, family requirements, etc.

The surveyed MLS librarians were asked to rate how well they thought their library and information science (LIS) education prepared them for (1) their initial assignment and (2) their current position. Ratings were 1 = not at all well to 7 = extremely well. (See the Web Extra supplement for comments concerning how well education prepared MLS librarians for their work. The comments are arranged by ratings [1 to 7] and by preparation for initial assignment or current position.) Generally, average ratings of preparedness were higher for their initial assignment than for their current position (4.60 vs. 4.31). This suggests that education may not prepare librarians as well for potential advanced positions as for their initial ones (see table 7.6 and discussion below). Table 7.5 shows the ratings of how their education prepared librarians with different levels of experience.

MLS librarians with less than 10 years' experience indicate that their education did not prepare them as well for their initial assignment as those having more experience, and their rating is down some for their current position (i.e., average rating of 4.59 for those having less than 10 years' experience vs. 4.72 and 4.75 for those having 10 to 19 years and 20 years or more, respectively). Perhaps the education has deteriorated or has lagged the changes in the workplace. However, the respondents are only those remaining in libraries, which might have a bearing on the results.

Also, those with less than 10 years' experience rate their preparation for the current position higher than those having more experience (i.e., 4.50, 4.22, and 4.21,

Table 7.5
Proportion (%) and Average Ratings of How Well Library and Information Science Education Prepared Surveyed MLS Librarians for Their Initial Assignment and Current Position, by Years of Experience: 2007 (n = 960)

Initial or Current Assignment	Years of Experience	RATINGS (%)			
		1 to 3: Not at All to Somewhat Well	4: Somewhat Well	5 to 7: Somewhat to Extremely Well	Average Rating
Initial Assignment	Less than 10 years	14.9	36.4	48.7	4.59
	10 to 19 years	15.0	30.7	54.3	4.72
	20 or more years	16.2	28.0	55.8	4.75
	All years	15.4	31.6	53.0	4.60
Current Position	Less than 10 years	18.5	32.8	48.7	4.50
	10 to 19 years	27.6	29.8	42.6	4.22
	20 or more years	28.4	31.4	40.2	4.21
	All years	25.0	31.3	43.7	4.31

University of North Carolina at Chapel Hill, School of Information and Library Science, for the Institute of Museum and Library Services

respectively). This is to be expected, since the workplace does change driven by both internal and external influences, and it is not possible in a one-year graduate program to anticipate all future needs. Similarly, those with 10 or more years of experience indicate that their education prepared them well for their initial assignment, but not as well for their current position.

Table 7.6 isolates these attitudes based on MLS librarians' level of employment. It is clear that there is a substantial drop-off in ratings of educational preparedness for administration as library directors, assistant or associate directors, and even as department or branch heads. In these positions the difference in average ratings from initial to current are −0.88, −0.75, and −0.56, respectively. Education for the first professional degree cannot completely prepare people for every position they might hold in the course of their careers, and the nature of the work itself changes over time. Nevertheless, those serving in another supervisory capacity generally rate their education less well than those continuing to work in a non-supervisory capacity.

Examination of the kind of operational work being done shows that satisfaction with educational preparation for the initial assignment and current position also varies a great deal. The ongoing debate related to the education of librarians is over the extent to which there is exposure to sufficient management/administrative content in the accredited MLS degree programs. Recently, new "executive MLS" programs have been considered and established. Like people in other professions, librarians need to recognize the importance of continuing education for career progress and keeping up with changes that affect the nature of the work (technologies, demographics of populations served, role of public institutions in their communities, etc.).

MLS librarians reported (Staff Survey) on additional education and training courses taken in the previous two years. More than one-fourth (26.2%) indicated they attended a university or college course, mostly at night (19.6%). Another 10.6

Table 7.6

Proportion (%) of MLS Librarians Who Indicated How Well Their Library or Information Science Education Prepared Them for Their Initial Assignment and Current Position, and Average Rating, by Their Current Level of Employment: 2007

Level of Employment	Sample (n)	EDUCATION PREPARATION FOR:	
		Initial Assignment	Current Assignment
Library director			
Well	62	61.3%	39.3%
Somewhat well		30.6%	31.1%
Not well		8.1%	29.5%
Average rating		5.03	4.15
Assistant/associate director			
Well	48	52.1%	31.3%
Somewhat well		27.1%	33.3%
Not well		20.8%	35.4%
Average rating		4.65	3.90
Department/branch head			
Well	297	52.2%	38.6%
Somewhat well		30.3%	39.5%
Not well		17.5%	31.9%
Average rating		4.60	4.04
Other supervisory capacity			
Well	119	46.2%	51.3%
Somewhat well		38.7%	32.0%
Not well		15.1%	16.7%
Average rating		4.55	4.24
Non-supervisory capacity			
Well	389	54.8%	43.7%
Somewhat well		31.1%	31.5%
Not well		14.1%	27.8%
Average rating		4.76	4.63

University of North Carolina at Chapel Hill, School of Information and Library Science, for the Institute of Museum and Library Services

percent indicated they attended a virtual university. Sometimes their courses were in pursuit of a degree. Nearly all said they attended at least one external workshop and internal formal training. Finally, about 10 percent attended a certificate of advancement class. (See the Web Extra supplement for reported topics covered in these education and training examples.) Also, see chapter 5 for an indication of how much public libraries spend in support of such education and training. It appears that not all education of MLS librarians is funded by public libraries.

PROGRESSION OF LEVEL AND TYPE OF EMPLOYMENT OF MLS LIBRARIANS

The years of experience working in a library gives some evidence of progression of primary level of employment, as shown in table 7.7. The progression is what might be expected, although 28.3 percent of MLS librarians remain in a non-supervisory capacity even though they have 20 or more years' experience. Later it is shown that many MLS librarians are not satisfied with their opportunities for advancement (see table 7.14 below).

Table 7.7

Proportion (%) of Surveyed Public MLS Librarians and Their Primary Level of Employment, by Ranges of Years of Experience in a Librarian Capacity: 2007 (n = 1,005)

Level of Employment	YEARS OF EXPERIENCE (%)		
	‹10 years	10 to 19 years	20 or more years
Director	2.1	4.0	12.2
Assistant or associate director	1.5	4.0	8.5
Department or branch head	21.6	39.3	33.4
Other supervisory capacity	12.5	13.4	10.8
Non-supervisory capacity	57.4	35.9	28.3
Other	4.9	3.4	6.8
Total	100.0	100.0	100.0

University of North Carolina at Chapel Hill, School of Information and Library Science, for the Institute of Museum and Library Services

Table 7.8

Proportion (%) of Surveyed Public MLS Librarians and the Departments to Which They Are Primarily Assigned, by Ranges of Years of Experience in a Librarian Capacity: 2007

Primary Department Assigned	YEARS OF EXPERIENCE (%)		
	‹10 years (n = 267)	10 to 19 years (n = 323)	20 or more years (n = 353)
Library not organized by department	7.5	6.5	6.1
Administration	4.0	10.9	23.9
Acquisitions	0.8	1.9	2.2
Technical services	4.9	8.5	6.2
User services	27.1	24.8	22.1
Reference and research	47.8	32.6	23.6
Special collections	0.4	1.2	0.7
Systems	0.8	1.9	2.5
Other (not specified)	14.2	18.2	18.8

University of North Carolina at Chapel Hill, School of Information and Library Science, for the Institute of Museum and Library Services

The progression in years of experience also reflects the departments in which librarians work, as shown in table 7.8. Interestingly, the proportions of librarians in most departments (or type of work done) remain about the same except reference and research, and to a lesser amount user services, in which proportions decrease substantially as years of experience increase. Administration increases appreciably by years of experience, which may mean the "path" to administration tends to be through reference and research or user services.

Fewer of the more experienced librarians work in libraries that are not organized by departments (i.e., probably small libraries). It may be that some move from small libraries (e.g., branches) to large libraries (e.g., central) as they progress in their careers.

CONTINUITY OF MLS LIBRARIANS

Eighty-five percent of current MLS librarians say they have remained employed in a public library since initial employment. The rest (15%) moved in and out of public library employment for various reasons, including illness or disability; went to work in another occupation; had family obligations (e.g., raise children); increase in positions or salary; relocation; to further education; military; library downsized, or librarian was laid off or quit; or some other reason. These reasons (for leaving and then returning) are presented in table 7.9 by gender, keeping in mind that the results represent only MLS librarians currently employed.

Table 7.9

Proportion (%) of Returning Public MLS Librarians by Reasons They Left the Library Workforce and Returned, by Gender: 2007

| | GENDER | | |
Reason Left the Workforce	Male (n = 13)	Female (n = 123)	Total (n = 136)
Illness or disability	0.0	0.8	0.7
Employed in another occupation	30.8	13.8	15.4
Family obligations	0.0	39.0	35.3
Increase in position/salary	0.0	3.3	3.0
Relocation	23.1	23.6	23.5
To further education	7.7	2.4	3.0
Military	0.0	0.8	0.7
Downsized, laid off, quit	15.4	4.9	5.9
Other	23.1	11.4	12.5
Total	100.1	100.0	100.0

Sums may exceed 100 percent due to rounding.

University of North Carolina at Chapel Hill, School of Information and Library Science, for the Institute of Museum and Library Services

There is a clear gender difference in those who left and then returned. For example, 39 percent of females left for family obligations. Males who left and returned were more likely to do so to be employed in another occupation or were downsized or laid off and then returned.

The Library Survey also provided some evidence of MLS librarians leaving the library workforce in 2007. This survey asked libraries to indicate information related to MLS librarians who left in the past year such as age, gender, reasons for leaving, etc. About 4 percent of MLS librarians (36,169) are reported to have left a public library to work in another type of library. Others are reported to have left for the reasons given in table 7.10 (see also chapter 8).

Excluding those who died and those who left because of illness or disability, there were 1,366 MLS librarians who left the library workforce and might come back later. Table 7.11 compares the proportion of these librarians estimated from the Library Survey with the proportion of librarians that came back as reported in the

Table 7.10
Number and Proportion (%) of Public MLS Librarians Who Left the Workforce: 2007 (n = 823)

Reason Left the Workforce	Number of MLS Librarians (n = 36,169)	PROPORTION (%)	
		All Librarians	Who Left Workforce
Death	126	0.3	4.6
Illness or disability	126	0.3	4.6
Retirement	1,230	3.4	45.2
Employed in another occupation	279	0.8	10.2
Family, education, military	179	0.5	6.6
Downsized, laid off	90	0.2	3.3
Other (unknown)	692	1.9	25.4
Total who left library workforce	2,722	7.4	99.9

University of North Carolina at Chapel Hill, School of Information and Library Science, for the Institute of Museum and Library Services

Table 7.11
Number and Proportion (%) of Public MLS Librarians Who Left the Workforce (not including those who died or retired): 2007 (n = 823)

Reason Left the Workforce	Staff Who Left and Came Back (%)	Staff Who Left (%)
Illness or disability	0.7	9.2
Employed in another occupation	15.4	20.4
Family, education, military	39.0	13.1
Downsized, laid off	5.9	6.6
Other (unknown)	39.0	50.7
Total	100.0	100.0

University of North Carolina at Chapel Hill, School of Information and Library Science, for the Institute of Museum and Library Services

Staff Survey. These data indicate that those who leave due to illness or disability are least likely to return (0.7%), and those who leave for family, education, or military service are most likely to return (39%); those employed in another occupation fell in the middle (15.4%).

The MLS librarians surveyed were asked if they had not retired and come back, at what age they anticipated retiring. The ages anticipated by MLS librarians and the ages of librarians who were reported to have actually retired in 2007 are given by gender in table 7.12. The age of anticipated retirement is somewhat older than that reported by those who actually retired. The anticipated age of retirement is not too different for males and females, but males tend to actually retire at an earlier age than females. This finding was confirmed in 2009 by Tordella and Godfrey.[1]

Some surveyed MLS librarians (4.3%) retired and came back to work in a library, often as a temporary employee or part-time. The age at which the librarians initially retired is given in table 7.13.

Table 7.12

Proportion (%) of Surveyed Public MLS Librarians Who Anticipate Retiring and Those Who Are Reported to Have Retired, by Gender and Age Group: 2007 (n = 823, n = 951)

Retirement Age Group	ANTICIPATED RETIREMENT AGE (%)			REPORTED RETIREMENT AGE (%)		
	Male	Female	Total	Male	Female	Total
40 to 50	1.6	1.1	1.2	—	2.5	2.1
51 to 55	8.8	6.2	6.6	28.6	12.8	15.1
56 to 60	17.6	17.8	17.7	31.4	24.6	25.6
61 to 65	41.6	45.0	44.5	37.1	40.9	40.3
Over 65	30.4	29.9	29.9	2.9	19.2	16.8

University of North Carolina at Chapel Hill, School of Information and Library Science, for the Institute of Museum and Library Services

Table 7.13

Proportion (%) of Surveyed Public MLS Librarians Who Retired and Came Back to Work in a Library, by Their Age When Retired: 2007 (n = 42)

Range of Age When Retired	Proportion of MLS Librarians Who Retired (%)
36 to 40	18.4
41 to 50	7.9
51 to 55	18.4
56 to 60	28.9
61 to 65	26.3
Total	99.9

University of North Carolina at Chapel Hill, School of Information and Library Science, for the Institute of Museum and Library Services

Some librarians indicated that they retired relatively young but decided to return to the library workforce. When one returns to work after retiring, one's work status often changes and salaries or wages change. In fact, 64.3 percent of those who retired returned as part-time employees (compared with 11.7% of those who have yet to retire), and 15 percent are considered temporary employees (vs. 1.5% for those not yet retired). The retiree average salaries are about two-thirds of others, although hourly wages are about the same ($20.20 for retirees vs. $18.60 per hour for those not yet retired).

One aspect of coming back to work part-time after retiring is the total compensation package, since part-time staff often do not receive some fringe benefits. For example, part-time retirees will likely not receive further retirement or pension benefits. In fact, 96.5 percent of MLS librarian full-time employees report these benefits available, whereas 72.2 percent of part-time employees do. Ninety-eight percent of full-time MLS librarians have employee medical insurance available, but only 56.8 percent of part-time librarians do, and 87.5 percent of full-time librarians have life insurance available versus 50 percent of part-time librarians. Thus, having part-time MLS librarians can result in substantial fringe-benefit cost savings for some public libraries, depending on their personnel policies and practices.

PUBLIC MLS LIBRARIAN ATTITUDES TOWARD WORK-RELATED ISSUES

MLS librarians were asked to rate (1 to 5) the importance of and their satisfaction with their salary, fringe benefits, type of work they do, opportunities for advancement, and geographic location. They also were asked, if they had the opportunity to choose their career over, would they still choose librarianship.

Ratings of importance (1 = very unimportant to 5 = very important) and satisfaction (1 = dissatisfied to 5 = very satisfied) are reported for work-related issues in table 7.14. Importance is generally rated much higher than satisfaction (the exception being geographic location). The greatest disparity between importance and satisfaction is with salary (0.75 difference in importance and satisfaction average rating), with fringe benefits second (0.44 difference in average rating).[2] Both of these issues involve forms of compensation. Opportunities for advancement is rated lowest in importance and satisfaction, while type of work done is highest, which is related to whether librarians would choose librarianship again if given an opportunity, as shown next.

MLS librarians were asked, if they could choose their career over again, would they still choose librarianship. The ratings in table 7.15 are: 1 = definitely not, 2 = probably not, 3 = unsure, 4 = probably, and 5 = definitely. The ratings are given for different years of experience. Roughly three-fourths of public MLS librarians (76.5%) say they would choose librarianship if they could choose their career again, regardless of years of experience. The 76.5 percent is compatible with 76.5 percent who said they are satisfied or very satisfied with the type of work done.

Satisfaction with work-related issues is related to whether or not librarians would choose librarianship if they had the opportunity to choose their careers over again, as shown in table 7.16. It appears that those who would definitely or probably not choose librarianship again as a career are mostly dissatisfied with their salary (2.36) and opportunity for advancement (2.42). Over 50 percent of those not

Table 7.14

Proportion (%) and Average Ratings (1 = low to 5 = high) of Importance of and Satisfaction with Work-Related Issues by Surveyed Public MLS Librarians: 2007 (n = 996)

| Work-Related Issues | Type of Rating | PROPORTION (%) | | | | | Average Rating |
		1	2	3	4	5	
Salary	Importance	4.5	0.8	7.5	58.9	28.2	4.05
	Satisfaction	8.6	22.6	11.8	44.3	12.7	3.30
Fringe benefits	Importance	4.5	2.0	10.7	52.9	29.9	4.02
	Satisfaction	7.3	12.8	13.0	48.3	18.7	3.58
Type of work done	Importance	6.0	—	1.4	25.5	67.1	4.48
	Satisfaction	1.8	7.2	4.5	29.5	47.0	4.23
Opportunities for advancement	Importance	4.5	8.2	31.2	40.9	15.2	3.54
	Satisfaction	10.5	13.8	30.5	35.3	9.8	3.20
Geographic location	Importance	4.8	2.2	11.3	49.1	32.5	4.02
	Satisfaction	2.3	9.2	8.8	39.6	40.1	4.06

University of North Carolina at Chapel Hill, School of Information and Library Science, for the Institute of Museum and Library Services

Table 7.15

Proportion (%) and Average Ratings of Whether Surveyed Public MLS Librarians Would Choose Librarianship Again as a Career, by Years of Experience: 2007 (n = 953)

| Years of Experience | PROPORTION OF RATINGS (%) | | | | | Average Rating |
| | (Definitely Not) | | | | (Definitely) | |
	1	2	3	4	5	
Less than 10 years	1.6	4.3	16.1	34.9	43.1	4.13
10 to 14 years	1.3	10.6	16.1	34.4	36.6	3.96
20 or more years	1.2	6.5	13.0	37.0	42.3	4.13
All years	1.4	7.1	15.0	35.5	41.0	4.08

University of North Carolina at Chapel Hill, School of Information and Library Science, for the Institute of Museum and Library Services

choosing librarianship again are either satisfied or very satisfied with the type of work they do, which suggests this is not a significant negative issue with current librarians; in fact, this is a very positive issue with public library work.

Opportunity for advancement and salary are somewhat linked as a function of level of employment. Librarian sentiment with librarianship as a career is examined by level of employment in table 7.17. The higher the position in a public library, the more often MLS librarians say they would again choose librarianship as a career. Surprisingly, those in other supervisory and non-supervisory capacities share similar attitudes toward choosing librarianship as a career.

Table 7.16

Proportion (%) and Average Ratings of Satisfaction (1 = low to 5 = high) with Salaries, Type of Work Done, and Opportunities for Advancement, by Whether Public MLS Librarians Would Choose Librarianship If They Had the Opportunity to Choose Their Career Again: 2007 (n = 987)

Work-Related Issues/Would Choose Librarianship	SATISFACTION RATINGS (%)					Average Rating
	1	2	3	4	5	
Salary						
Definitely/probably would	5.8	20.0	11.8	48.3	14.1	3.45
Unsure	12.9	26.5	12.2	40.1	8.2	3.04
Definitely/probably would not	25.3	41.0	9.6	20.5	3.6	2.36
Type of work done						
Definitely/probably would	0.7	4.4	2.5	39.1	53.4	4.40
Unsure	2.7	12.2	8.8	48.3	27.9	3.86
Definitely/probably would not	9.6	22.9	14.5	32.5	20.5	3.31
Opportunity for advancement						
Definitely/probably would	7.0	12.1	32.3	37.0	11.6	3.34
Unsure	14.6	20.1	27.8	32.6	4.9	2.93
Definitely/probably would not	33.3	17.3	25.9	21.0	2.5	2.42

University of North Carolina at Chapel Hill, School of Information and Library Science, for the Institute of Museum and Library Services

Table 7.17

Proportion (%) of Public MLS Librarians Who Would or Would Not Choose Librarianship Again as a Career, by Level of Employment: 2007 (n = 986)

Level of Employment	WOULD CHOOSE LIBRARIANSHIP AGAIN (%)			
	Sample (n)	Definitely/ Probably Would	Unsure	Definitely/ Probably Would Not
Library director	69	85.5	11.6	2.9
Assistant/associate director	47	78.7	12.8	8.5
Department/branch head	301	77.4	14.6	8.0
Other supervising capacity	122	73.0	17.2	9.8
Non-supervising capacity	396	75.0	15.2	9.8
Other	51	82.4	15.7	1.9

University of North Carolina at Chapel Hill, School of Information and Library Science, for the Institute of Museum and Library Services

The department primarily assigned (i.e., type of work) is examined in table 7.18. It appears that MLS librarians currently in administration and user services are more likely to choose librarianship again as a career, but those in acquisitions are least likely to.

Table 7.18

Proportion (%) of Public MLS Librarians Who Would or Would Not Choose Librarianship Again as a Career, by the Department Primarily Attached: 2007

Department Primarily Attached	WOULD CHOOSE LIBRARIANSHIP AGAIN (%)			
	Sample (n)	Definitely/ Probably Would	Unsure	Definitely/ Probably Would Not
Administration	103	82.5	15.5	1.9
Acquisitions	14	64.3	14.3	21.4
Technical services	50	74.0	20.0	6.0
User services	193	80.8	10.4	8.8
Reference and research	244	69.7	19.3	11.0
Systems	14	71.4	14.3	14.3
Other	129	76.7	15.5	7.8

University of North Carolina at Chapel Hill, School of Information and Library Science, for the Institute of Museum and Library Services

Notes

1. Stephen Tordella and Thomas Godfrey, *Planning for 2015: The Recent History and Future Supply of Librarians* (2009). A report prepared for the American Library Association's Senior Management and Executive Board to inform its 2015 strategic planning activities. Compiled by Denise M. Davis. www.ala.org/ala/research/librarystaffstats/recruitment/Librarians_supply_demog_analys.pdf.

2. Both the importance of and satisfaction with work-related issues can affect work and/or continued work in libraries. The worst situation is when importance is rated highly and satisfaction is very low.

TEN-YEAR FORECAST OF THE NUMBER OF PUBLIC MLS LIBRARIANS IN THE WORKFORCE

C hapters 6 and 7 presented data and information from several sources that referred to past trends in the number of MLS librarians in the public library workforce, where they fit in the library staff structure, type of work done, salaries and fringe benefits, and career paths. This chapter presents a 10-year forecast of the future demand for MLS librarians, and chapter 9 describes the effects of the past and current recessions on the MLS librarian workforce, services, and budgets. This chapter ends with a 2009 study by Tordella and Godfrey that also projects to 2015 the number of librarians by age groups.

The 10-year forecast of MLS librarians is based on three measures. The first is a forecast of the total number of MLS librarians who are expected to be in the workforce over ten years starting in 2007–08 and ending in 2016–17. The second measure is the attrition that is expected in 2007–08 and each additional year, including 2016–17. Attrition occurs from death, illness, retirement, and other reasons why MLS librarians leave the workforce (and sometimes return). Each year the number of MLS librarians who leave (and some who come back) is subtracted from the ending number for the previous year. Finally, the current vacancies are added to the workforce in the first year. The total demand for new MLS librarians after ten years is determined by adding attrition each year, filled vacancies, and additional librarians that are expected each year.

The forecast of the expected number of MLS librarians over ten years was made by the economist Joel Popkin using econometric modeling of past NCES data. (Details of this model are given in the Web Extra supplement.) The attrition measures are based on U.S. census death rates by age and gender applied to current MLS librarians. Data related to other reasons for leaving are based on a combination of the 2007 Library and Staff surveys. Reasons for leaving are based on asking the libraries in the Library Survey to indicate how many MLS librarians left in the past year, the reasons each left, their age and gender, etc. An estimate of the number who left and returned is based on asking MLS librarians in the Staff Survey whether they had left the library workforce, if so, why, and for how long.

The analysis of these data is similar to an actuarial analysis. The analysis is based on a range of the number of MLS librarians categorized by age and gender. Each subsequent year the numbers in each category are advanced one year to adjust for the increase in age. Then estimates are applied for those who leave and return.

ESTIMATE OF THE TEN-YEAR DEMAND FOR MLS LIBRARIANS

Adding total attrition, current vacancies that need to be filled, and the expected number of new public librarians yields an estimate of total demand for public MLS librarians over ten years. *The total attrition from the beginning workforce (36,169) is 21,165 MLS librarians, the number of vacancies is 1,408 MLS librarians, and the expected number of new positions is 3,745 MLS librarians, resulting in a 10-year demand for 26,318 new MLS librarians* (i.e., 21,165 + 1,408 + 3,745). Details of this analysis are described below step-by-step.

ESTIMATE OF THE NUMBER OF CURRENT MLS PUBLIC LIBRARIANS (HEAD COUNT)

The first step is to estimate the number of MLS public librarians (head count) in 2007. The NCES provides estimates of the total full-time equivalent (FTE) MLS librarians. For example, there were estimated to be 30,873 FTE MLS librarians in 2005. It is necessary to convert the number of FTE librarians to a head count of MLS librarians because the survey of librarians and any future estimates of the workforce must take into account full-time, as well as part-time, librarians. First, the public libraries are stratified by the number of in-person visits as a proxy (i.e., substitute) measure of the size of libraries. The numbers of FTE librarians in 2005 (based on NCES) are given in table 8.1 by ranges of annual in-person visits.

Also in table 8.1 are estimates of the proportions of MLS librarians who are currently employed full-time or part-time, based on the 2007 Staff Survey. For example, there are 18,565.43 FTE librarians in libraries that have 500,000 or more in-person visits. Of these, 91.2 percent are estimated to be full-time and 8.8 percent part-time (i.e., the 1,634 FTE part-time librarians). The Staff Survey also provides data on the number of hours worked in a standard workweek by full-time and part-time librarians, which in turn provides a means to estimate the total head count. Since part-time librarians spend about half-time, the 1,634 part-time FTE converts to a 3,268 head count added to the 16,932 FTE full-time, giving a total head count of 20,200 (rounded).

Table 8.1 shows that there were estimated to be 34,936 MLS librarians (head count) in 2005–06. Using established methods for estimating future growth based

Table 8.1
MLS Librarian Head Count Estimated from Number of MLS Full-Time Equivalents (NCES, 2005): 2007

Number of Visits	MLS Librarians FTE	Full-Time (%)	Part-Time (%)	Head Count Full-Time	Head Count Part-Time	Total Head Count 2005	Total Head Count 2007
Less than 4,999	44.63	91.7	8.3	41	7	48	50
5,000 to 9,999	87.42	72.0	28.0	63	49	112	116
10,000 to 24,999	358.84	72.0	28.0	258	201	459	476
25,000 to 49,999	795.52	92.3	7.7	734	122	857	887
50,000 to 99,999	1,663.34	68.6	31.4	1,141	1,046	2,186	2,263
100,000 to 249,999	4,488.83	79.8	20.2	3,584	1,809	5,394	5,584
250,000 to 499,999	4,869.14	83.3	16.7	4,058	1,623	5,681	5,881
500,000 or more	18,565.43	91.2	8.8	16,932	3,268	20,199	20,912
Total	30,873.15	—	—	26,811	8,125	34,936	36,169

University of North Carolina at Chapel Hill, School of Information and Library Science, for the Institute of Museum and Library Services

on prior performance, Popkin determined that the total average annual growth was 0.0175 (or 1.75%) for MLS librarians per year. Therefore, advancing two years to 2007–08, the head count of MLS librarians is estimated to be 36,169, assuming that FTE and head counts both increase at a constant rate from 2005–06 to 2007–08.

FORECASTS OF THE EXPECTED NUMBER OF MLS PUBLIC LIBRARIANS: 2007–08 TO 2016–17

The demand for library services grew noticeably during the period from 1992 to 2005. While population grew at a 1.3 percent annual rate, library visits grew more than twice as fast, at 2.9 percent annually, according to data from annual censuses conducted until recently under the aegis of the NCES. In order to assess the sustainability of such usage growth, it was necessary to evaluate how visits are affected by change in population mix, particularly age distribution.

Not all services may result in the same increment of demand for MLS librarians. Thus, circulation grew at a 2.2 percent rate and reference transactions grew even more slowly at a 1.8 percent rate as compared with the growth of visits. Interlibrary loan activities (incoming and outgoing) grew at double-digit rates. It is instructive to note that the rate of growth of library staff (1.75 percent) was most closely correlated with that of reference transactions. Staff growth during the period was about the same for all types of staff (librarians and other staff).

The economic projection of the expected number of MLS public librarians is given as a straight declining projection of growth at a rate of 0.0175 (or 1.75%) in 2007–08 from 2006–07 down to 0.0037 (or 0.37%) in 2016–17 as given in table 8.2, based on correlation of declining reference transactions. Applying these straight-line

Table 8.2

Expected Growth of MLS Librarians from 2007–08 to 2016–17

Beginning of Year	Rate of Growth	Projection of MLS Librarians	Increase during Year
2007	0.01612	36,169	583
2008	0.01474	36,752	542
2009	0.01336	37,294	498
2010	0.01198	37,792	453
2011	0.01060	38,245	405
2012	0.00922	38,650	357
2013	0.00784	39,007	305
2014	0.00646	39,312	254
2015	0.00508	39,566	201
2016	0.00370	38,767	147
2017	—	30,014	—
Total	—	—	3,745

University of North Carolina at Chapel Hill, School of Information and Library Science, for the Institute of Museum and Library Services

projections (i.e., a declining rate of 0.00138 each year), there should be 3,745 more MLS librarians in the workforce in 2016–17 than in 2006–07.

ESTIMATE OF THE ATTRITION OF MLS LIBRARIANS WHO LEFT THE PUBLIC LIBRARY WORKFORCE IN 2007–08

The 2007 Staff Survey provides categories of surveyed MLS librarians by age and gender. Table 8.3 displays the 951 responses to these categories and estimates the 2007–08 total head count of MLS librarians (36,169). These data are important because attrition is highly dependent on age and gender. For example, death rates and retirement are substantially different for males and females and by age.

The 2007 Library Survey provided 823 responses reporting MLS librarians leaving the public library workforce, categorized by their age and gender. Table 8.4 displays the sample responses projected to the total 4,256 MLS librarians who are estimated to have left the workforce in the past 12 months (2007). For example, there are estimated to be 3,583 females (11.8% of all female MLS librarians) who left and 672 males (11.5%) who left (again, small differences are due to carrying calculations forward without rounding).

These gender-specific estimates are applied to the number of MLS librarians. When asked reasons why librarians left the workforce, an equal number of libraries cited "death" and "illness or disability," making it possible to combine the response categories and provide a single number who left for "death, illness, or disability" reasons. Table 8.5 displays those estimates, along with the remaining number of MLS librarians. Altogether, 35,917 librarians remain after the attrition of 252 due to these reasons.

Table 8.3

Estimate of Number of MLS Librarian Head Count, by Age and Gender: 2007–08 (n = 951)

Age	NUMBER SURVEYED			PROJECTION TO TOTAL HEAD COUNT		
	Female	Male	Total	Female	Male	Total
‹25	19	—	19	723	—	723
26–30	85	10	95	3,233	380	3,613
31–35	93	26	119	3,537	989	4,526
36–40	88	31	119	3,347	1,179	4,526
41–45	82	22	104	3,119	837	3,955
46–50	88	12	100	3,347	456	3,803
51–55	153	24	177	5,819	913	6,732
56–60	137	19	156	5,211	723	5,933
61–65	43	6	49	1,635	228	1,864
›65	9	4	13	342	152	494
Total	797	154	951	30,312	5,857	36,169

Projection totals may vary from detail due to computer calculations that must be carried forward in developing estimates.

University of North Carolina at Chapel Hill, School of Information and Library Science, for the Institute of Museum and Library Services

Table 8.4

Estimate of Number of MLS Librarian Head Count Who Left Libraries in the Past 12 Months, by Age and Gender: 2007 (n = 823)

Age	NUMBER SURVEYED			PROJECTION TO TOTAL HEAD COUNT		
	Female	Male	Total	Female	Male	Total
‹25	26	5	31	134	26	160
26–30	91	13	104	470	67	537
31–35	74	14	88	383	72	455
36–40	80	16	96	414	83	497
41–45	64	16	80	331	83	414
46–50	55	13	68	284	67	351
51–55	76	18	94	393	93	486
56–60	84	17	101	434	88	522
61–65	97	16	113	502	83	585
›65	46	2	48	238	10	249
Total	693	130	823	3,583	672	4,256

Projection totals may vary from detail due to computer calculations that must be carried forward in developing estimates.

University of North Carolina at Chapel Hill, School of Information and Library Science, for the Institute of Museum and Library Services

Table 8.5

Estimate of Number of MLS Librarians Who Are Likely to Leave Public Libraries Due to Death, Illness, or Disability; and the Remaining Number of MLS Librarians, by Age and Gender: 2007 (n = 823)

Age	LIKELIHOOD DUE TO DEATH, ILLNESS, OR DISABILITY			DO NOT LEAVE		
	Female	Male	Total	Female	Male	Total
21–25	1	—	1	722	—	722
26–30	4	1	5	3,229	379	3,608
31–35	5	3	7	3,533	986	4,519
36–40	10	6	15	3,337	1,173	4,511
41–45	9	4	13	3,110	833	3,942
46–50	21	5	26	3,326	451	3,777
51–55	37	10	46	5,782	903	6,685
56–60	74	16	90	5,137	706	5,843
61–65	23	5	28	1,612	223	1,835
>65	12	8	20	330	144	474
Total	194	58	252	30,118	5,799	35,917

Projection totals may vary from detail due to computer calculations that must be carried forward in developing estimates.

University of North Carolina at Chapel Hill, School of Information and Library Science, for the Institute of Museum and Library Services

Table 8.6

Projection of MLS Librarians Who Left Public Libraries, by Reasons and by Gender: 2007–08 (n = 823)

Reason	PROPORTION (%) SURVEYED WHO LEFT			PROJECTED NUMBER WHO LEFT		
	Female	Male	Total	Female	Male	Total
Retirement	30.9	29.8	30.7	1,050	179	1,230
Employment in another library	37.0	45.5	38.3	1,260	274	1,533
Employment in another occupation	7.0	6.6	7.0	239	40	279
Dropped out of library workforce because of family, education, military, etc.	5.1	0.8	4.5	174	5	179
Library downsize or laid off	2.2	2.5	2.2	75	15	90
Other (specify)	17.7	14.9	17.3	602	90	692
Total	100.0	100.0	100.0	3,400	602	4,003

Projection totals may vary from detail due to computer calculations that must be carried forward in developing estimates.

University of North Carolina at Chapel Hill, School of Information and Library Science, for the Institute of Museum and Library Services

The Library Survey also provides evidence of other reasons why MLS librarians left in the past 12 months (2007–08) and which can be projected to the total number of those who left (less those who left due to death, illness, or disability). The projections of reasons are given in table 8.6. Altogether, 1,230 librarians are estimated to have left for retirement; 1,533 to go to another library; 279 to enter another occupation; 179 dropped out for family, education, or military purposes, etc.; and about 90 left because the library downsized or they were laid off. An estimated 692 left for unspecified reasons.

The age and gender of MLS librarians who retired is estimated from the Library Survey, providing a total estimate of about 3.1 percent of current male MLS librarians and 3.5 percent of female librarians retiring in 2007–08. A higher proportion of females than males retired later than age 65 (19.2% vs. 2.9%).

A total of 1,533 librarians are estimated to go from a public library to employment in another library. It is assumed that these librarians remain in the public library workforce, or at least the number who go to another type of library might be replaced by librarians from another type of library, based on an earlier study.[1] This number (1,533) of librarians is ignored in further estimates since there is an even exchange of staffing and no net reduction in the public librarian workforce.

All other reasons are aggregated, including those employed in another occupation (279), dropped out because of family, etc. (179), library downsized (90), or other (692) for a total of 1,240 librarians. This number is subtracted from the remaining number of public librarians, as shown in table 8.7. For example, a total of 1,090 female librarians (3.6%) and 149 male librarians (2.5%) are estimated to leave for other reasons. These data, when subtracted from the remaining number of librarians, result in estimates of the number of MLS public librarians who did not leave the

Table 8.7

Estimate of the Number of MLS Librarians Who Left Public Libraries Due to Employment in Another Occupation, Family, Education, Military Service, Downsized or Laid Off, or Other Reasons and the Remaining Number, by Age and Gender: 2007–08 (n = 823)

Age	PROPORTION (%) WHO LEFT FOR OTHER REASONS		TOTAL NUMBER WHO LEFT FOR OTHER REASONS			MLS LIBRARIANS REMAINING		
	Female	Male	Female	Male	Total	Female	Male	Total
‹25	8.9	3.3	97	5	102	625	—	625
26–30	17.8	13.3	194	20	214	3,034	359	3,394
31–35	16.3	13.3	178	20	198	3,354	966	4,321
36–40	18.3	20.0	200	30	230	3,138	1,143	4,281
41–45	12.9	23.3	140	35	175	2,964	798	3,762
46–50	6.9	13.3	76	20	95	3,230	432	3,661
51–55	10.9	3.3	119	5	124	5,529	847	6,376
56–60	3.5	3.3	38	5	43	4,840	645	5,485
61–65	3.0	6.7	32	10	42	1,150	147	1,297
›65	1.5	—	16	—	16	112	139	251
Total	100.0	100.0	1,090	149	1,240	27,977	5,475	33,452

Projection totals may vary from detail due to computer calculations that must be carried forward in developing estimates.

University of North Carolina at Chapel Hill, School of Information and Library Science, for the Institute of Museum and Library Services

public library workforce in the past 12 months (2007–08). This means that of 36,169 MLS librarians, a total of 2,717 left, leaving 33,452 who remain in the public library workforce. (Note that there are some minor differences in rounded numbers that vary from computer calculations that carry over detailed data. For example, the total in rounded numbers is 33,447 remaining.)

Further, the 2007 Staff Survey provides estimates of the proportion of MLS librarians who left the public library workforce and came back, the reasons for leaving, and the length of time they were away. About 4.69 percent of females and 8.33 percent of males who left in 2007–08 for other reasons are estimated to have returned in that year or later. About 51 MLS librarians left and then returned in that year, meaning that there were 33,503 MLS librarians at the end of the first year (i.e., 33,452 + 51).

SUBSEQUENT ATTRITION OF MLS LIBRARIANS WHO LEFT THE WORKFORCE (2008–09 TO 2016–17)

Estimating the attrition of the public librarian workforce is impacted by three factors: aging, exit, and reentry within that year, and exit and reentry within more than one year.

It is estimated that there were 33,503 MLS public librarians remaining in 2007–08, but in 2008–09 the age of these librarians advanced by one year, as shown in table 8.8. Each age range is five years, therefore one-fifth of those in each age range move up into the next higher age range each year. For example, the 628 females under 25 years old in 2007–08 decrease by about 126, leaving about 503 (rounded) remaining in 2008–09 in this category. Those 3,042 females aged 26–30 decrease by 609 but increase by 126 of those previously in the 21–25 age category, leaving 2,559 females aged 26–30 in 2008 (i.e., 3,042 − 609 + 126).

Table 8.8
Estimate of Number of MLS Librarians Who Advanced One Year in Age from 2007–08 to 2008–09, by Age Category and Gender

Age	NUMBER OF MLS LIBRARIANS IN 2007–08			NUMBER OF MLS LIBRARIANS IN 2008–09		
	Female	Male	Total	Female	Male	Total
25 and under	628	—	628	486	—	486
26–30	3,042	361	3,402	2,576	289	2,865
31–35	3,361	967	4,329	3,297	846	4,143
36–40	3,145	1,145	4,290	3,188	1,110	4,298
41–45	2,969	800	3,770	3,005	869	3,874
46–50	3,232	433	3,665	3,180	506	3,686
51–55	5,534	847	6,381	5,073	764	5,838
56–60	4,842	645	5,487	4,980	686	5,666
61–65	1,152	147	1,299	1,890	247	2,136
>65	113	139	252	343	168	512
Total	28,018	5,485	33,503	28,018	5,485	33,503

Projection totals may vary from detail due to computer calculations that must be carried forward in developing estimates.

University of North Carolina at Chapel Hill, School of Information and Library Science, for the Institute of Museum and Library Services

Subsequent change from 2008–09 to 2016–17 requires a similar analysis as above for each year. However, as shown above, the values in the categorization of age and sex are different each year because current librarians get one year older. Many of the other 2,671 MLS librarians, who left but did not come back in 2007–08, did come back later. The number of librarians who leave and come back increases by one year each year. For example, some librarians who left in 2007–08 will come back in 2008–09, in addition to those who left in 2008–09 and came back that year. The Staff Survey provided evidence to include the number who leave and the year they come back.

The next analysis is to estimate the attrition of the beginning workforce (36,169 as noted in table 8.3) through the 10-year period. For example, in 2007–08 an estimated 2,722 MLS librarians left the workforce and 51 came back in that year, leaving an attrition of 2,671 MLS librarians in that year. Attrition estimates for the years 2007–08 through 2016–17 are given in table 8.9. Results show that a total of 21,929 librarians left and 3,224 returned the first time for a total attrition of the beginning workforce (36,169) of 18,705 MLS librarians.

As mentioned earlier in this chapter, there were 1,408 MLS librarian vacancies at the beginning of 2007–08 (see also table 6.5). It is assumed that these vacancies will be filled in the first year. However, as with other librarian positions, some that are filled will leave and come back in 2007–08.[2] This number is estimated to be 104 librarians (see table 8.10). The beginning workforce attrition in 2007–08 is 2,671 plus the attrition for the filled vacancies (104) who might return and leave again: 26 for the beginning and 1 for the filled vacancies, resulting in a total of 2,802 total attrition (i.e., 2,671 + 104 + 26 + 1).

Table 8.9
Number of Beginning Public MLS Librarians Who Left for Various Reasons and Those Who Returned in Years 2007–08 to 2016–17

| Year | REASONS FOR LEAVING | | | Total Who Left | Total Who Returned | Beginning Workforce Attrition |
	Death and Illness	Retired	Other Reason			
2007–08	252	1,230	1,240	2,722	51	2,671
2008–09	243	1,262	1,116	2,621	164	2,457
2009–10	234	1,274	1,016	2,525	99	2,426
2010–11	223	1,253	922	2,398	368	2,030
2011–12	212	1,212	848	2,272	420	1,852
2012–13	201	1,156	781	2,139	412	1,727
2013–14	190	1,093	719	2,002	446	1,556
2014–15	180	1,029	662	1,871	439	1,432
2015–16	171	966	609	1,746	431	1,315
2016–17	162	908	563	1,633	394	1,239
Total	2,068	11,383	8,476	21,929	3,224	18,705

University of North Carolina at Chapel Hill, School of Information and Library Science, for the Institute of Museum and Library Services

Table 8.10

Beginning Public MLS Librarian Workforce Attrition, Attrition from Vacancies, and Follow-on Attrition by Years 2007–08 to 2016–17

Year	Beginning Workforce Attrition	2007–08 Vacancy Attrition	FOLLOW-ON ATTRITION		Total Attrition
			Beginning	Vacancies	
2007–08	2,671	104	26	1	2,802
2008–09	2,457	96	85	3	2,641
2009–10	2,426	94	51	2	2,573
2010–11	2,030	79	190	7	2,306
2011–12	1,852	72	217	9	2,150
2012–13	1,727	67	213	8	2,015
2013–14	1,556	61	231	9	1,857
2014–15	1,432	56	227	9	1,724
2015–16	1,315	51	223	9	1,598
2016–17	1,239	48	204	8	1,499
Total	18,705	728	1,667	65	21,165

University of North Carolina at Chapel Hill, School of Information and Library Science, for the Institute of Museum and Library Services

Some of the 51 beginning librarians who had left and returned in 2007–08 are likely to leave again and not return over the next nine years. This number is 26 MLS librarians, which is referred to as "beginning follow-on attrition" in table 8.10. Similarly, the number of librarians who left and returned to fill vacancies in 2007–08 and who are also likely to leave again permanently is estimated to be one MLS librarian. These results are determined each year by the length of time reported by MLS librarians. The numbers over the next nine years are given in table 8.10 and add up to 728 vacancy attrition, 1,667 beginning follow-on attrition, and 65 follow-on vacancy attrition. The total attrition is 21,165 MLS librarians over ten years.

TOTAL 10-YEAR DEMAND OF MLS LIBRARIANS (2007–08 TO 2016–17)

Total demand is found by adding up the total attrition (see table 8.10), vacancies, and expected additional positions. These values are 2,802, 1,408, and 583 librarians, respectively, for 2007–08, with the following years given in table 8.11. The total 10-year demand is estimated at 26,318 public librarians. Therefore, in the absence of abnormal times or events, one would expect there to be a 10-year demand for 26,318 new MLS librarians from 2007–08 to 2016–17.

The 10-year forecast of public MLS librarians represents the best data we could find, but such forecasts are challenging for the following reasons:

▌ The demand for public MLS librarians is related to the supply provided by LIS programs accredited by the ALA, and there is evidence that the number of MLS graduates may not meet the demand.

Table 8.11
Total Public MLS Librarian Demand by Source of Demand by Years 2007–08 to 2016–17

Year	Total Attrition	Current Vacancies	Expected New Positions	Total Demand
2007–08	2,802	1,408	583	4,793
2008–09	2,641	—	542	3,183
2009–10	2,573	—	498	3,071
2010–11	2,306	—	453	2,759
2011–12	2,150	—	405	2,555
2012–13	2,015	—	357	2,372
2013–14	1,857	—	305	2,162
2014–15	1,724	—	254	1,978
2015–16	1,598	—	201	1,799
2016–17	1,499	—	147	1,646
Total	21,165	1,408	3,745	26,318

University of North Carolina at Chapel Hill, School of Information and Library Science, for the Institute of Museum and Library Services

▌ With the current economic turmoil, projecting workforce needs even in the short term is difficult at best and especially so with workforce needs in sectors tied closely to the economy.

▌ Future workforce needs may not be similar to current needs.

▌ Current job conditions, as well as projections about future workforce needs, influence individuals' decisions, thereby altering the future demand and supply.

Despite the difficulty in forecasting workforce needs, the information and data provide a benchmark from which to test from time to time in the future. The IMLS, ALA, and other relevant parties can examine pertinent indicators such as MLS graduates entering the public library workforce, changes in the number of public libraries, library staff structure, departures from the workforce, and so on.

The 10-year forecast of the number of MLS librarians appears to be reasonable, even in light of past experiences of national recessions (see chapter 9). In those recessions, in which each covered four years, the number of librarians increased 3.5 percent from 1978 to 1982, 21.6 percent from 1990 to 1994, and 3.7 percent from 2000 to 2004. However, the current recession (2008 to 2010) may not be a typical recession in that unemployment has been higher than usual in recessions and the stock market plunged much lower than in the past, requiring an unusual anti-recession federal response.

The current recession may have some consequences that could be favorable to the MLS librarian workforce: (1) more persons out of work will apply to graduate schools, providing a more healthy supply of new librarians, and (2) more MLS librarians will remain in the workforce due to fewer job opportunities elsewhere and delayed retirements. Public librarians appear to ride out recessions better than many professions. However, one important consideration is the future of public library revenue sources (discussed in chapter 5).

Similar results were observed by Stephen Tordella and Tom Godfrey in 2009. They started by examining the "bubble" of librarians in their 50s and projected the number of librarians in ranges of age from 2005 to 2015, as shown below. This demographic study conducted for the ALA by Tordella and Godfrey using 36 years of census data determined that 41 percent of librarians were in their 50s, creating a librarian "bubble" of baby boomers. Figure 8.1 presents the progression of librarians from 1980 to 2006; figure 8.2 presents the baby boomer bubble; and figure 8.3 presents projections to 2015 for the librarian labor force.[3]

Notes

1. M. D. Cooper, N. A. Van House, and N. K. Roderer, King Research, Inc., *Library Human Resources: A Study of Supply and Demand* (Chicago: American Library Association, 1983).

2. The attrition of the beginning 1,408 vacancies is 104, based on 106 who left and two who returned in 2007–08.

3. American Library Association, "Planning for 2015: The Recent History and Future Supply of Librarians," 2009, www.ala.org/ala/research/librarystaffstats/recruitment/Librarians_supply_demog_analys.pdf.

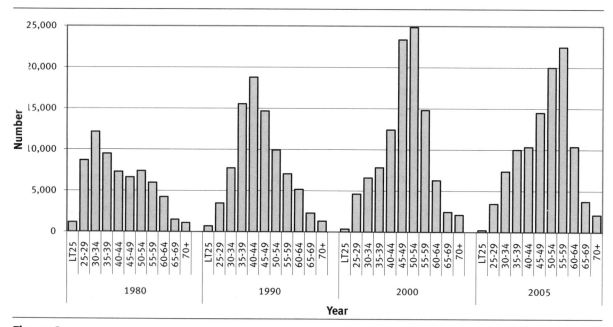

Figure 8.1
Number of Credentialed Librarians, by Age, 1980–2005

Ten-Year Forecast of the Number of Public MLS Librarians in the Workforce

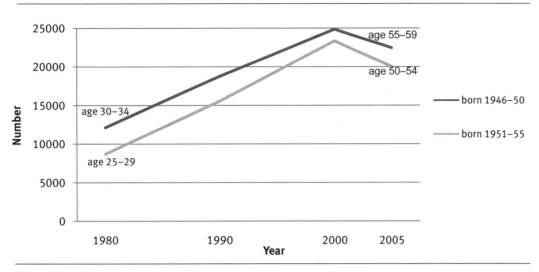

Figure 8.2

Tracking Baby Boom Credentialed Librarians, 1980–2005

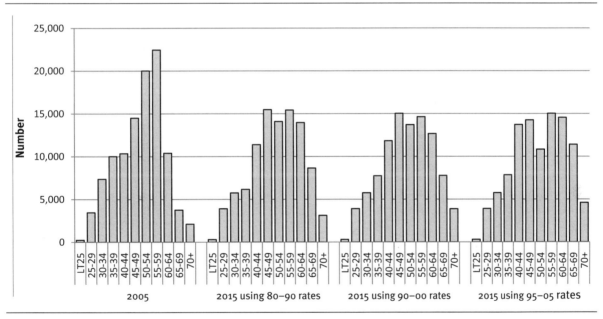

Figure 8.3

Number of Credentialed Librarians in 2005 and 2015, Projected Using Results from Three Past Time Periods

LIBRARIAN EMPLOYMENT AND LIBRARY EXPERIENCE DURING THE PAST THREE RECESSIONS (1978–2004)

There have been three significant recessions in recent decades for which the library community has corresponding data with which to determine their effects on library services and librarian employment. These recessions are

- The early 1980s, when there were two economic troughs in January 1980 and November 1982. Average unemployment rates ranged from 5.8 percent in 1979 to 9.7 percent in 1982.

- The early 1990s, when the trough was in March 1991 and unemployment went from 5.6 percent in 1990 to 7.5 percent in 1992 and back to 6.1 percent in 1994.

- The early 2000s, when the trough was in November 2001 and unemployment went from 4 percent in 2000 to 6 percent in 2003 and down to 5.5 percent in 2004.

The current recession began in 2008 and is ongoing. In late 2009 a study[1] was funded by the ALA and the Bill and Melinda Gates Foundation to provide the most current national information available on public library funding and technology use and services. The FY 2009–2010 study involved a survey of public libraries (n = 7,393, an 82.4% response rate) and 46 responses to a state library agency survey (90% response rate).

The national unemployment rate for 1978 to 2010 is given in figure 9.1. The figure shows the unemployment rate from 1978 to 2010, including during the last three recessions. In terms of unemployment during these three recessions, the one in the early 1980s appears to be much more severe, with the peak in unemployment being 9.7 percent in 1982 following the troughs in January 1980 and November 1982, versus 7.5 percent in 1992 following the economic trough in March 1991 and 6 percent

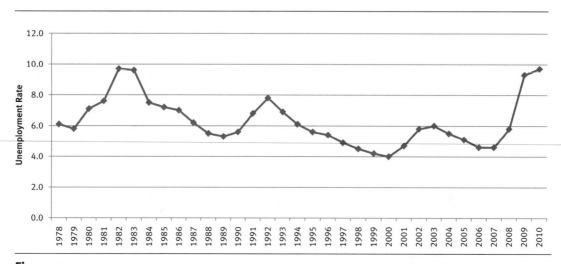

Figure 9.1
U.S. Unemployment Rate (%), 1978–2010

in 2003 following the economic trough in November 2001. The observations during these recessions begin with the year unemployment rates started up and extend for four additional years.

Public librarian employment is found to increase during the three past recessions, but not on a per-capita basis, in which a small decline is observed. During recessions public libraries generally experience a decline in income from state, federal, and other sources, but continue to remain stable or show growth due to local taxation (where income is adjusted by population served and inflation). Salaries and wages represent as much as 70 percent of library operating expenditures and increase during recessionary periods, but collection and other expenditures decline. Even in light of this experience, visits and some service uses increase during recessions and do not drop following the recessions, suggesting that increased use stimulates use that might not be experienced otherwise. Public libraries are shown to deal with recessions by closing some outlets (e.g., branches and bookmobiles), reducing some types of expenditures, and cutting back on hours of opening. Data are provided below to demonstrate these assertions.[2]

PUBLIC LIBRARIAN EMPLOYMENT DURING THREE RECESSIONS

This part focuses on public librarian employment during the early 1980s, 1990s, and 2000s recessions. Data are provided by an NCES-sponsored survey from the years 1978 through 1982 which covers the early 1980s recession.[3] Tables are given for total number of public librarians; other professional positions; and technical, clerical, and other support staff. Data covering the latter two recessions are provided by NCES reports (now available through the IMLS). In particular, tables give the size of paid staff (MLS librarians, other librarians, and non-librarians), size of staff per 10,000 population served, and national unemployment rates for the years 1990 to 1994 and 2000 to 2004.[4] Additional estimates beyond the NCES results are provided for the years 2002 and 2007 and results based on the 2007 Library Survey.[5]

EMPLOYMENT OF PUBLIC LIBRARY STAFF DURING THE EARLY 1980S RECESSION

The early 1980s recession was the most severe of the three past recessions in terms of national unemployment rates, inflation, and gross national product. This recession had business troughs in 1980 and 1982, and national unemployment rates ranged from 6.1 percent to 9.7 percent. Table 9.1 gives survey estimates of staff for the four-year period from 1978 to 1982. All three types of staff increased during these years, but librarians the least (3.5%).

The absolute change from 1978 to 1982 is about 1,050 more public librarians. Although not reflected in this table, public libraries also lost 220 librarians in the last year (1982) because more of them became employed in other types of libraries than the number who migrated from other libraries to public libraries. Further, about 160 more public librarians left to work as information professionals than those who came to public libraries from the information profession. Finally, the supply of educated librarians decreased sharply during this time, with new MLS librarians declining from 6,080 in 1977 to 4,200 in 1981 and other librarians with a master's degree declining from 1,230 to 770 over the same time period. This undoubtedly severely dampened the hiring of public librarians.

Some changes in the number of public librarians are affected by increases in population and the subsequent effect on increased use of services, which is discussed later. For this reason the library staff are examined in the context of the national

Table 9.1

Size of Public Library Staff (FTE),[1] by Type of Staff, during the Early 1980s Recession: 1978–1982

Year	Unemployment Rate (%)[2]	SIZE OF STAFF (FTE)			
		All Staff	Librarians	Other Professionals	Support[3]
1978	6.1	77,810	30,050	3,990	43,770
1979	5.8	77,570	29,890	4,280	43,400
1980[4]	7.1	78,960	30,410	4,320	44,230
1981	7.6	78,600	30,720	4,300	43,580
1982[4,5]	9.7	82,150	31,100	4,290	46,760
4-year change	—	+5.6%	+3.5%	+7.5%	+6.8%

1. M. D. Cooper, N. A. Van House, and N. K. Roderer, King Research, Inc. *Library Human Resources: A Study of Supply and Demand, 1983*. A librarian is defined as "a library staff member doing work that requires professional training and skill in the theoretical and/or scientific aspect of library work, as distinct from its mechanical or clerical aspect. While a librarian will normally possess a Master's in Library Science or equivalent degree, . . . librarians are defined by their job responsibilities rather than educational qualifications."

2. U.S. Bureau of Labor Statistics, http://data.bls.gov/cgi-bin/print.pl/cps/prev_yrs.htm.

3. Technical, clerical, and other support staff positions.

4. National Bureau of Economic Research, Inc., "Business Cycle Expansions and Contractions," www.nber.org/cycles.htm.

5. 1978–1981 data were reported directly as totals by survey respondents, while 1982 data were calculated as the sum of full-time employees plus full-time equivalency (FTE) of part-time employees plus unfilled positions.

University of North Carolina at Chapel Hill, School of Information and Library Science, for the Institute of Museum and Library Services

Table 9.2

Size of Public Library Staff (FTE)[1] per 10,000 Total Population, by Type of Staff, during the Early 1980s Recession: 1978–1982

Year	Unemployment Rate (%)[2]	SIZE OF STAFF PER 10,000 TOTAL POPULATION			
		All Staff	Librarians	Other Professionals	Support[3]
1978	6.1	3.50	1.35	0.18	1.97
1979	5.8	3.45	1.33	0.19	1.93
1980 [4]	7.1	3.45	1.34	0.19	1.94
1981	7.6	3.42	1.34	0.19	1.90
1982[4,5]	9.7	3.54	1.34	0.18	2.02
4-year change		+1.1%	−0.7%	—	+2.5%

1. M. D. Cooper, N. A. Van House, and N. K. Roderer, King Research, Inc. *Library Human Resources: A Study of Supply and Demand, 1983*. A librarian is defined as "a library staff member doing work that requires professional training and skill in the theoretical and/or scientific aspect of library work, as distinct from its mechanical or clerical aspect. While a librarian will normally possess a Master's in Library Science or equivalent degree, . . . librarians are defined by their job responsibilities rather than educational qualifications."

2. U.S. Bureau of Labor Statistics, http://data.bls.gov/cgi-bin/print.pl/cps/prev_yrs.htm.

3. Technical, clerical, and other support staff positions.

4. National Bureau of Economic Research, Inc., "Business Cycle Expansions and Contractions," www.nber.org/cycles.htm.

5. 1978–1981 data were reported directly as totals by survey respondents, while 1982 data were calculated as the sum of full-time employees plus full-time equivalency (FTE) of part-time employees plus unfilled positions.

University of North Carolina at Chapel Hill, School of Information and Library Science, for the Institute of Museum and Library Services

population (see table 9.2). From this perspective the public library staff grow very little and the number of librarians per 10,000 population actually decreases slightly (−0.7%).

EMPLOYMENT OF PUBLIC LIBRARY STAFF DURING THE EARLY 1990S RECESSION

The NCES reports the size of public library staff by MLS librarians, other librarians, and other paid staff. Table 9.3 gives the NCES estimates of the size of public library staffs during the early 1990s recession (1990–94). All staff categories increased (4.3%) during this period, with MLS librarians increasing the most (21.6%) and the number of other librarians actually decreasing (5.5%) from 12,800 in 1990 to 12,100 in 1994.

When the population served by public libraries (i.e., the population in the legal service areas) is considered (table 9.4), the MLS librarians continue to show a substantial increase per 10,000 population served (14.8%), other librarians show a 9.4 percent decrease from 0.53 other librarians per 10,000 population in 1990 to 0.48 in 1994, and other paid staff show a decline of 4.2 percent, which contributes to a decline of all staff per 10,000 population.

Table 9.3

Size of Public Library Staff (FTE), by Type of Staff, during the Early 1990s Recession: 1990–1994

Year	Unemployment Rate (%)	SIZE OF PAID STAFF (000)[1]			
		All Staff	MLS Librarians	Other Librarians	Other Paid Staff
1990	5.6	108.2	21.3	12.8	73.2[2]
1991	6.8	108.0	23.4	11.1	73.5
1992	7.5	109.9	24.5	11.5	73.9
1993	6.9	111.9	24.8	12.5	74.6
1994	6.1	112.8	25.9	12.1	74.8
4-year change	—	+4.3%	+21.6%	−5.5%	+2.2%

1. Estimates are based on reported data and may be underestimated due to non-responses that vary from year to year.

2. National Center for Education Statistics (now provided by Institute of Museum and Library Services), *Public Libraries in the United States*.

University of North Carolina at Chapel Hill, School of Information and Library Science, for the Institute of Museum and Library Services

Table 9.4

Size of Public Library Staff (FTE) per 10,000 Population Served, by Type of Staff, during the Early 1990s Recession: 1990–1994

Year	Unemployment Rate (%)	SIZE OF PAID STAFF PER 10,000 POPULATION SERVED[1]			
		All Staff	MLS Librarians	Other Librarians	Other Paid Staff
1990	5.6	4.47	0.88	0.53	3.06
1991	6.8	4.26	0.92	0.44	2.90
1992	7.5	4.52	1.01	0.47	3.04
1993	6.9	4.29	0.95	0.48	2.86
1994	6.1	4.42	1.01	0.48	2.93
4-year change	—	−1.1%	+14.8%	−9.4%	−4.2%

1. Estimates are based on reported data and may be underestimated due to non-responses that vary from year to year.

National Center for Education Statistics (now provided by Institute of Museum and Library Services), *Public Libraries in the United States*.

University of North Carolina at Chapel Hill, School of Information and Library Science, for the Institute of Museum and Library Services

EMPLOYMENT OF PUBLIC LIBRARY STAFF DURING THE EARLY 2000S RECESSION

As during the early 1990s recession, the NCES provides estimates of public library staff size for the duration of the early 2000s recession, as shown in table 9.5. All staff increased 4.5 percent and the increases do not vary greatly by type of staff; that is, 3.7 percent for MLS librarians, 5.9 percent for other librarians, and 4.6 percent for other paid staff.

Table 9.5

Size of Public Library Staff (FTE), by Type of Staff, during the Early 2000s Recession:
2000–2004

Year	Unemployment Rate (%)	SIZE OF PAID STAFF (000)			
		All Staff	MLS Librarians	Other Librarians	Other Paid Staff
2000	4.0	130.1	29.5	13.6	87.0
2001	4.7	133.5	30.1	14.3	89.1
2002	5.8	136.2	30.4	14.5	91.3
2003	6.0	136.2	30.5	14.6	91.1
2004	5.5	136.0	30.6	14.4	91.0
4-year change	—	+4.5%	+3.7%	+5.9%	+4.6%

National Center for Education Statistics (now provided by Institute of Museum and Library Services), *Public Libraries in the United States.*

University of North Carolina at Chapel Hill, School of Information and Library Science, for the Institute of Museum and Library Services

Table 9.6

Size of Public Library Staff (FTE) per 10,000 Population Served, by Type of Staff,
during the Early 2000s Recession: 2000–2004

Year	Unemployment Rate (%)	SIZE OF PAID STAFF PER 10,000 POPULATION SERVED			
		All Staff	MLS Librarians	Other Librarians	Other Paid Staff
2000	4.0	4.80	1.09	0.50	3.21
2001	4.7	4.79	1.08	0.51	3.20
2002	5.8	4.86	1.09	0.51	3.26
2003	6.0	4.79	1.08	0.51	3.19
2004	5.5	4.74	1.07	0.50	3.17
4-year change	—	−1.3%	−1.8%	—	−1.2%

National Center for Education Statistics (now provided by Institute of Museum and Library Services), *Public Libraries in the United States.*

University of North Carolina at Chapel Hill, School of Information and Library Science, for the Institute of Museum and Library Services

The staff size adjusted by the population served (legal service area) shows a small decrease for MLS librarians and other paid staff, but no change for other librarians at 0.50 per 10,000 population in 2000 and 2004 (see table 9.6).

FURTHER EVIDENCE OF EMPLOYMENT OF PUBLIC LIBRARIANS

Davis and Hall summarize NCES estimates of public librarians from 1989 to 2004.[6] The interesting aspect of these results is the employment of librarians in the five years (1995 to 1999) between the latter two recessions, as shown in table 9.7.

Table 9.7
Number of Public Librarians from 1995 to 1999, and Trend Compared with the Early 1990s and Early 2000s Recessions

Year	Unemployment Rate (%)	TYPE OF LIBRARIAN (FTE)		
		All Librarians	MLS Librarians	Other Librarians
1995	5.6	38,694	26,636	12,058
1996	5.4	39,095	27,353	11,742
1997	4.9	40,161	27,946	12,215
1998	4.5	40,689	28,178	12,511
1999	4.2	41,772	28,822	12,950
4-year change (%)		**+8.0%**	**+8.2%**	**+7.4%**
1990	5.6	34,082	21,305	12,777
1994	6.1	38,048	25,879	12,169
4-year change (%)[1]		**+11.6%**	**+21.5%**	**−4.8%**
2000	4.0	43,118	29,519	13,599
2004	5.5	45,037	30,560	14,477
4-year change (%)[1]		**+4.5%**	**+3.5%**	**+6.5%**

1. D. M. Davis and T. D. Hall, "Diversity Counts," American Library Association.

University of North Carolina at Chapel Hill, School of Information and Library Science, for the Institute of Museum and Library Services

While the employment of MLS librarians has increased during the three recessions (which is encouraging), it appears that the positive trend in their employment has declined over a 15-year period (i.e., 21.5% from 1990 to 1994; 8.2% from 1995 to 1999; and 3.5% from 2000 to 2004). Some of this decline in the rate of increase might be due to changes in age characteristics and retirement, while some may be due to changes in the supply of MLS librarians to the public library workforce, which appears to experience increasing competition from employment demands in other types of libraries and other employment options. Also, the trend in employment of other librarians may take jobs that MLS librarians might otherwise fill.

The 2007 Library Survey[7] provides estimates from a survey of public libraries' staff size (head count) in 2002 and 2007. These estimates (table 9.8) show an increase of 9.4 percent in the employment of MLS librarians (head count). In 2005 the NCES estimated that there were 30,873 full-time equivalent MLS librarians, which included 26,811 full-time and 8,125 part-time MLS librarians, or a head count of 34,936. Therefore, the mix of full-time and part-time staff can influence trends in employment measured as full-time equivalents.

The IMLS report on public libraries[8] reports that "public libraries had a total of 145,000 paid full-time equivalent staff in FY 2007, an increase of 5,000 over the previous year. There were 12.4 paid FTE staff persons per 25,000 people in FY 2007, virtually the same as there were in FY 2006 (12.2 FTE). Library staffing levels have been fairly stable during the study time period ranging from 11.9 (FY 1998) to a high of 12.4 in FY 2007." Note that the staff levels in table 9.8 are higher because they represent head count, not FTE.

Table 9.8
Size of Public Library Staff (Head Count) Estimated from a 2007 Survey of Public Libraries, by Type of Staff: 2002, 2007

Year	Unemployment Rate (%)	TYPE OF STAFF (Head Count)			
		All Staff	MLS Librarian	Professional Working as Librarian	Non-Librarian
2002	5.8	164,739	33,074	9,277	122,388
2007	4.6	181,622	36,169	9,549	135,904
5-year change (%)		+10.2%	+9.4%	+2.9%	+11.0%

J. M. Griffiths and D. W. King, "A National Study of the Future of Public Librarians in the Workforce," 2009.

University of North Carolina at Chapel Hill, School of Information and Library Science, for the Institute of Museum and Library Services

The U.S. Bureau of Labor Statistics (BLS) provides estimates of the number of librarians in the United States where librarians (occupational code 25–4021) are defined by what they do, but not by educational requirements.[9] Based on the BLS National Employment Matrix describing occupations in 2006 and 2016, it is estimated that the number of librarians working in local government (excluding education and hospitals) was 42,242 in 2006 and is expected to increase to 42,708 in 2016, an increase of only 1.1 percent. Most of these librarians surely work in public libraries, but could also work in libraries found in local government agencies.

EXPERIENCE OF PUBLIC LIBRARIES DURING THE LAST TWO RECESSIONS

Recessions affect all sectors of the economy, including employment, sources of funds, expenditures, and so on. This section addresses the experience of public libraries during the two past recessions, since NCES data are only available since 1990. These experiences include potential changes in the number of public libraries (central, branch, and bookmobiles) during the early 1990s recession (1990–94) and early 2000s recession (2000–04); changes in library income sources (in constant dollars per capita) and in expenditures (also in constant dollars per capita); changes in the average number of weekly public service hours per outlet; and changes in the number of visits and some services provided per capita. The effect of the recessions on staff sizes was shown above.

Recessions can potentially affect all sources of public library income because of tightened sector budgets, which in turn could result in closing of libraries, reduced staff sizes and expenditures, shortened library hours, and reduced service provision. On the other hand, recessions also result in general population unemployment and lower salaries and wages, which potentially could increase demand for public library services because adults have more time on their hands; they use library services to support job hunting, further their education, look for ways to reduce household expenditures, examine financial issues, and so on; and they save money on purchases of books and other materials. This section attempts to address these issues through observation of the two most recent recessions, those in the early 1990s and early 2000s.

NUMBER OF PUBLIC LIBRARIES DURING TWO RECESSIONS

The number of central public libraries is reported by the NCES. The NCES shows a decline and then a rise in the number of public libraries in the early 1990s recession, so that it was the same in 1990 and 1994 at 8,876. The number increased from 8,921 in 1995 to 9,046 in 1999 and steadily increased from 9,074 in 2000 to 9,211 in 2003, but declined to 9,198 in 2005. It was reported to be 9,214 central libraries in 2007.

A further examination is provided by the type of libraries involved, including central and branch libraries and bookmobiles. Central and branch libraries are stationary outlets. Some bookmobiles are included as an outlet in the total number of libraries (tables 9.9 and 9.10). The general population increased 5.4 percent during the early 1990s recession (1990–94) and 5.8 percent during the early 2000s recession (2000–04). The total number of public libraries[10] decreased slightly during the early 1990s recession (–0.6%) and increased somewhat during the early 2000s recession (+1.5%), but not nearly as rapidly as the general population. Branch libraries followed the total and central library trends in the latter recession, but increased faster than the population in the early 1990s. Bookmobiles decreased nearly every year during the recessions, likely as an economic measure, but continued downward from 1994 to 2000 (i.e., 996 bookmobiles to 884, respectively) at the start of the second recession and further so to 2004. The number of public libraries has increased about 13 percent over a 25-year period from 8,140 central libraries in 1982 to 9,214 in 2007 and recently from 9,137 in 2002. While the reported number has not increased each year, the number increased in most years.

Table 9.9

Population Served by Public Libraries and Number of Public Libraries during the Early 1990s Recession: 1990–1994

Year	Population[1] (millions)	NUMBER OF PUBLIC LIBRARIES[1]			
		Total	Central	Branch	Bookmobile
1990	242.4	8,978	8,876	6,562	1,102
1991	253.6	9,050	8,940	6,542	1,125
1992	243.3	8,946	8,837	7,035	1,066
1993	261.1	8,929	8,887	7,017	1,035
1994	255.5	8,921	8,876	7,024	996
4-year change	+5.4%	–0.6%	—	+7.0%	–9.6%

1. Estimates are based on reported data and may be underestimated due to non-responses that vary from year to year.

National Center for Education Statistics (now provided by Institute of Museum and Library Services), *Public Libraries in the United States.*

University of North Carolina at Chapel Hill, School of Information and Library Science, for the Institute of Museum and Library Services

Table 9.10

Population Served by Public Libraries and Number of Public Libraries during the Early 2000s Recession: 2000–2004

Year	Population (millions)	NUMBER OF PUBLIC LIBRARIES			
		Total	Central	Branch	Bookmobile
2000	270.9	9,074	8,915	7,383	884
2001	278.8	9,129	8,971	7,450	879
2002	280.4	9,137	8,986	7,500	873
2003	283.5	9,211	9,062	7,479	864
2004	286.7	9,207	9,047	7,502	844
4-year change	+5.8%	+1.5%	+1.5%	+1.6%	−4.5%

National Center for Education Statistics (now provided by Institute of Museum and Library Services), *Public Libraries in the United States.*

University of North Carolina at Chapel Hill, School of Information and Library Science, for the Institute of Museum and Library Services

PUBLIC LIBRARY SOURCES OF REVENUE AND EXPENDITURES DURING TWO RECESSIONS

This section discusses public library revenues and expenditures during the last two recessions. Some evidence is given concerning the current recession. The total revenue was $4.32 billion in 1990 and $11 billion in 2007. The revenues for 1994 were $5.26 billion (i.e., a 21.8% increase from 1990). From 2000 to 2004 the total revenues increased from $7.03 billion to $9.13 billion (a 29.9% increase).

Total expenditures increased from $4.07 billion in 1990 to $10.21 billion in 2007. During the 1990s recession expenditures rose from $4.07 billion to $4.93 billion in 1994 (a 21.1% increase), and from 2000 to 2004 they rose from $7.03 billion to $8.64 billion (a 22.9% increase).

PUBLIC LIBRARY OPERATING INCOME DURING TWO RECESSIONS

The NCES reports estimates of public library income from local, state, federal, and other sources. The incomes given below are adjusted by the population served (legal service area) and in constant dollars starting with the initial year of the relevant recession period. The results of this analysis are given for the two recession periods in tables 9.11 and 9.12. The trend in adjusted incomes was much more favorable in the early 1990s recession than the latter one, even though the recession was more severe. That is, total adjusted income was slightly up in the early 1990s (+1.8%) and down in the early 2000s (−1.9%). In both instances, income from state, federal, and other sources was down, and particularly severely during the early 2000s. Thus, the local source of income has carried public libraries in terms of absolute amounts and continued positive trends. This may not bode well for the current recession because many public libraries are funded through property taxes, and this recession was triggered by bad mortgages and foreclosures.

Table 9.11

Total Operating Income per Capita (in Constant 1990 Dollars) of Public Libraries, by Source of Income, during the Early 1990s Recession: 1990–1994

Year	Population (millions)	OPERATING INCOME PER CAPITA ($)[1]				
		Total	Local	State	Federal	Other
1990	242.4	17.83	13.51	2.49	0.23	1.60
1991	253.6	17.63	13.54	2.31	0.21	1.58
1992	243.3	17.83	15.04	2.29	0.20	1.61
1993	261.1	17.57	13.70	2.20	0.19	1.47
1994	255.5	18.15	14.20	2.23	0.20	1.53
4-year change	+5.4%	+1.8%	+5.1%	−10.4%	−13.0%	−4.4%

1. Estimates are based on reported data and may be underestimated due to non-responses that vary from year to year.

Projection totals may vary from detail due to computer calculations that must be carried forward in developing estimates.

National Center for Education Statistics (now provided by Institute of Museum and Library Services), *Public Libraries in the United States.*

University of North Carolina at Chapel Hill, School of Information and Library Science, for the Institute of Museum and Library Services

Table 9.12

Total Operating Income per Capita (in Constant 2000 Dollars) of Public Libraries, by Source of Income, during the Early 2000s Recession: 2000–2004

Year	Population (millions)	OPERATING INCOME PER CAPITA ($)				
		Total	Local	State	Federal	Other
2000	270.9	28.96	22.31	3.70	0.21	2.73
2001	278.8	28.81	22.26	3.67	0.16	2.71
2002	280.4	28.85	22.81	3.36	0.16	2.51
2003	283.5	28.85	23.07	3.14	0.16	2.48
2004	286.7	28.41	23.15	2.83	0.15	2.28
4-year change	+5.8%	−1.9%	+3.8%	−23.5%	−28.6%	−16.5%

Projection totals may vary from detail due to computer calculations that must be carried forward in developing estimates.

National Center for Education Statistics (now provided by Institute of Museum and Library Services), *Public Libraries in the United States.*

University of North Carolina at Chapel Hill, School of Information and Library Science, for the Institute of Museum and Library Services

EVIDENCE OF INCOME DURING THE CURRENT RECESSION

The ALA reports a decline in funding between FY 2009 and FY 2010,[11] with 24 states reporting cuts in state funding for public libraries and nearly half indicating the cuts were greater than 11 percent. This is almost four times the number reported in the previous fiscal year. However, 11 states said there were no changes and 3 indicated an increase in funding. Cuts at the state level were compounded by cuts at the local level, where a majority of states reported decreases in the 5 to 10 percent range.

The "Public Library Funding & Technology Access Study" described earlier provides some further evidence of declining sources of funding. The libraries reported sources of funds in 2008–2009 (i.e., FY 2008) and anticipated sources in FY 2009. An estimated CPI increase of 2.368 points is used to establish change in constant dollars. (The "points" are found by dividing the CPI value of the most recent year of interest by the first year of interest.) While showing an overall increase in funding (3.1%), these results are rather contrary to the two previous recessions in that local/county funding made up for substantial declines in funding from state, federal, and other sources. The change in constant dollars from FY 2008 to FY 2009 was negative for both local/county (–2.7%) and state sources (–4.7%), but up considerably for federal (+22%) and other sources (+16.9%). To put a perspective on these sources in FY 2009, local/county sources account for 56.5 percent of funding, state 8.8 percent, federal 1.7 percent, and other 33 percent.

In 2003, at the height of the last recession, these proportions were local (80%), state (10.9%), federal (0.6%), and other (8.6%). Clearly, funding has shifted from local to other sources of funding, which are largely made up of private foundation grants (47% of other sources of funds) and donations and local fund-raising (32.2%). Grants increased 31.2 percent in constant dollars and donations and local fund-raising increased 13 percent, accounting for most of the other funding sources. It is problematic that other sources can continue such positive increases in the future, and over a third of state library agencies (17 states) believed a majority of libraries in their states had received cuts in funding in FY 2010 compared with FY2009, although 21 percent (10 states) reported there had been no change between the two fiscal years. Two states reported funding increases. Others were uncertain.

TREND IN PUBLIC LIBRARY EXPENDITURES DURING TWO RECESSIONS

The NCES reported operation expenditures, which are also adjusted by population served and constant dollars. The results are given in tables 9.13 and 9.14. The expenditures somewhat follow income, although during both recessions the trend was positive, with the early 1990s recession having a more positive trend. The most striking result is that staff expenditures are by far the highest compared with collection and other expenditures, and also in comparison with the most positive trend in constant dollars per capita.[12] The fact that collection expenditures are particularly down contradicts the fact that circulation per capita is well up, as shown below in tables 9.14 (expenditures) and 9.19 (circulation).

The 2007 Library Survey of public libraries provides some reported trends in expenditures from 2002 to 2007.[13] The surveyed public libraries were asked to report their expenditures and general trend in expenditures in 2007 compared to five years ago (2002). Table 9.15 suggests a very positive trend for total expenditures and for salaries and wages, with a less positive trend for collections. It is noted that these results ignore increases in population served and adjustments for inflation, thereby presenting a different picture than given above.

Table 9.13

Total Operating Expenditures per Capita (in Constant 1990 Dollars) of Public Libraries, by Type of Expenditures, during the Early 1900s Recession: 1990–1994

Year	Population[1] (millions)	OPERATING EXPENDITURES PER CAPITA[1] ($)			
		Total	Staff	Collection	Other
1990	242.4	16.28	10.19	2.64	3.45
1991	253.6	17.02	10.84	2.62	3.56
1992	243.3	17.36	11.23	2.64	3.49
1993	261.1	16.30	10.65	2.44	3.21
1994	255.5	17.02	11.66	2.28	3.08
4-year change	+5.4%	+4.5%	+14.4%	−13.6%	−10.7%

1. Estimates are based on reported data and may be underestimated due to non-responses that vary from year to year.

National Center for Education Statistics (now provided by Institute of Museum and Library Services), *Public Libraries in the United States.*

University of North Carolina at Chapel Hill, School of Information and Library Science, for the Institute of Museum and Library Services

Table 9.14

Total Operating Expenditures per Capita (in Constant 2000 Dollars) of Public Libraries, by Type of Expenditures, during the Early 2000s Recession: 2000–2004

Year	Population (millions)	OPERATING EXPENDITURES PER CAPITA ($)			
		Total	Staff	Collection	Other
2000	270.9	26.42	16.96	4.02	5.44
2001	278.8	26.52	16.99	4.02	5.52
2002	280.4	26.96	17.44	3.89	5.46
2003	283.5	27.70	18.23	3.86	5.62
2004	286.7	26.89	17.69	3.56	5.64
4-year change	+5.8%	+1.8%	+4.3%	−11.4%	+3.7%

Projection totals may vary from detail due to computer calculations that must be carried forward in developing estimates.

National Center for Education Statistics (now provided by Institute of Museum and Library Services), *Public Libraries in the United States.*

University of North Carolina at Chapel Hill, School of Information and Library Science, for the Institute of Museum and Library Services

EVIDENCE OF EXPENDITURES DURING THE CURRENT RECESSION

There is also some evidence of declining expenditures during the current recession. The average public library operating expenditures reported by the ALA in the "Perfect Storm" brief are listed by type of expenditures for FY 2008 and FY 2009. The distribution of expenditures is similar to the past recession; for example, salaries account for 64.1 percent of expenditures compared with 65.8 percent in 2003 at the height of unemployment; collections account for 13.4 versus 13.9 percent; and other

Table 9.15

Annual Expenditures per Public Library, by Type of Expenditure, in 2007 and Trend Compared to Five Years Ago

Type of Expenditure	Sample (n)	Expenditure per Library (000)	TREND (%)				
			Down		Flat	Up	
			>10%	0 to 10%		0 to 10%	>10%
Total	1,848	$565	2.2	5.8	12.2	47.8	32
Salaries and wages	1,834	$372	1.5	3.9	10.1	53.4	31
Other	—	$193	—	—	—	—	—

	Sample (n)	Expenditure per Library (000)	Less		Same Now	More	
			Much	Somewhat		Somewhat	Much
Print collection	324	$41	5.9	13.2	22.9	46.9	11.1
Electronic collection	308	$6	3.5	4.4	34.8	30.8	26.4
Other collection	300	$13	3.4	6.9	36.8	38.7	14.2
Technology and system	380	$115	3.1	3.9	26.8	41.2	25.0
Outsourcing	225	$3	3.0	3.0	71.3	11.9	10.9
Other operating	281	$15	1.7	6.5	16.0	53.2	22.5

J. M. Griffiths and D. W. King, "A National Study of the Future of Public Librarians in the Workforce," 2009.

University of North Carolina at Chapel Hill, School of Information and Library Science, for the Institute of Museum and Library Services

expenditures account for 22.5 versus 20.3 percent. Collection expenditures appear to be in better shape in the current recession than in past recessions, perhaps due to the substantial rise in circulation observed during all recessions. The proportion of libraries reporting decreases in a public library system's operating budgets was consistently up from the previous year in FY 2009 compared with FY 2008, and increases were consistently down. Again, declining expenditures appear to be evident.

TREND IN PUBLIC LIBRARY VISITS AND SERVICES DURING TWO RECESSIONS

The trend for in-person visits is given here for the years 1990 to 2007. The total number of visits to public libraries was 507 million in 1990[14] and 1.43 billion in 2007. During the two recessions the visits increased from 507 million in 1990 to 820 million in 1994 and from 1.15 billion in 2000 to 1.32 billion in 2004 (a 14.8% increase). Details concerning visits are discussed below.

The NCES and IMLS report the number of visits per population served (legal service area). There was a sharp rise in visits during the early 1990s recession, a flattening out, and then another rise during the 2000s recession. The increases appear to coincide with the two recessions, with little or no drop-off off between recessions.

During the first recession (1990s) visits were almost exclusively in-person, with some contacts made by telephone. However, later visits began to be made remotely through the Internet. The IMLS commissioned the 2007 Library Survey, which provides some insight concerning in-person visits, as well as visits to libraries' websites and use of libraries' databases.[15]

Based on the 2007 Library Survey, the estimated average number of in-person visits per library, visits per hour of opening, and 2007 trend compared to five years ago are given in table 9.16. Clearly, in-person visits were reported to increase substantially by the responding public libraries.

An even greater trend is observed for remote visits to library websites and database use in table 9.17; the average visits per in-person visit are given because it is thought that these visits are correlated with in-person visits, as discussed below and in chapter 2.

Evidence of the positive relationship between in-person and remote online visits to public libraries is provided by a 2006 Telephone Survey of adults 18 and over, as reported in chapter 2.

The discussion below deals with circulation, reference transactions, interlibrary borrowing, circulation of children's materials, and children's program attendance during two recessions. Total circulation, reference transactions, and interlibrary borrowing are given below.

Table 9.16

Total Annual In-Person Visits per Public Library and Average Visits per Hour in 2007, and Trend Compared to Five Years Ago

Type of Visit	Sample (n)	Average Visits per Library (000)	Average Visits per Hour	TREND (%)				
				Down			Up	
				>5%	0 to 5%	Flat	0 to 5%	>5%
In-person	1,222	130.0	45.0	4.3	8.3	9.9	30.2	47.3

J. M. Griffiths and D. W. King, "A National Study of the Future of Public Librarians in the Workforce," 2009.

University of North Carolina at Chapel Hill, School of Information and Library Science, for the Institute of Museum and Library Services

Table 9.17

Total Annual Visits to Library Website and Database Use per Public Library, Average Visits per In-Person Visit, and Trend Compared to Five Years Ago: 2007

Type of Visit	Sample (n)	Average Visits per Library (000)	Average Visits per In-Person Visit	TREND (%)				
				Down			Up	
				>5%	0 to 5%	Flat	0 to 5%	>5%
Library website	2,035	100	0.72	1.7	1.5	4.0	35.0	57.0
Library's database	1,969	13	0.08	1.2	2.1	10.7	37.3	48.0

J. M. Griffiths and D. W. King, "A National Study of the Future of Public Librarians in the Workforce," 2009.

University of North Carolina at Chapel Hill, School of Information and Library Science, for the Institute of Museum and Library Services

Total circulation was reported to be as follows:

1990—1.39 billion	2004—2.01 billion
1994—1.57 billion	2007—2.17 billion
2000—1.71 billion	

The circulation increase during the early 1990s recession was 12.9 percent and was 17.5 percent in the early 2000s recession. The most recent result shows an increase to 2.17 billion in 2007.

The total reported reference transactions were as follows:

1990—209 million	2004—304 million
1994—258 million	2007—293 million
2000—291 million	

The 1990s recession increase in reference transactions was 12.7 percent, and the 2000s recession increase was 4.5 percent. However, reference transactions dropped to 293 million in 2007.

The total number of items borrowed was as follows:

1990—5.36 million	2004—30.47 million
1994—8.64 million	2007—49.97 million
2000—16.26 million	

Increases in items borrowed from other libraries were 61.2 percent in the early 1990s recession and 87.4 percent in the early 2000s.

These services are adjusted by the population served (legal service area) to provide a more meaningful comparison over the years. Tables 9.18 and 9.19 show the population served (legal service area) and per-capita increases in visits, circulation,

Table 9.18

Number of Public Library Visits, Circulation, Interlibrary Borrowing (ILB), and Reference Transactions per Capita during the Early 1990s Recession: 1990–1994

Year	Population (millions)	Visits per Capita[1]	Circulation per Capita[1]	Reference Transactions per Capita[1]	ILB per 1,000[1]
1990	242.4	3.1	5.8	0.9	22.1
1991	253.6	3.7	6.1	1.0	25.9
1992	243.3	4.0	6.4	1.0	29.9
1993	261.1	4.0	6.5	1.1	32.7
1994	255.5	4.1	6.4	1.1	35.1
4-year change	+5.4%	+32.3%	+10.3%	+19.6%	+58.8%

1. Estimates are based on reported data and may be underestimated due to non-responses that vary from year to year.

National Center for Education Statistics (now provided by Institute of Museum and Library Services), *Public Libraries in the United States.*

University of North Carolina at Chapel Hill, School of Information and Library Science, for the Institute of Museum and Library Services

Table 9.19
Number of Public Library Visits, Circulation, Interlibrary Borrowing (ILB), and Reference Transactions per Capita during the Early 2000s Recession: 2000–2004

Year	Population (millions)	Visits per Capita	Circulation per Capita	Reference Transactions per Capita	ILB per 1,000
2000	270.9	4.3	6.4	1.1	61.1
2001	278.8	4.3	6.5	1.1	70.5
2002	280.4	4.5	6.8	1.1	84.1
2003	283.5	4.5	6.9	1.1	93.8
2004	286.7	4.7	7.1	1.1	107.5
4-year change	+5.8%	+9.3%	+10.9%	—	+75.9%

National Center for Education Statistics (now provided by Institute of Museum and Library Services), Public Libraries in the United States.

University of North Carolina at Chapel Hill, School of Information and Library Science, for the Institute of Museum and Library Services

reference transactions, and number of items borrowed from other libraries. Circulation per capita increased over 10 percent during each of the two recessions, and interlibrary borrowing increased 58.8 percent in the 1990s recession and even more in the early 2000s recession (75.9%). Circulation flattened out between 1994 and 2000, suggesting the lasting positive influence of recessions on this service. This phenomenon is of interest because expenditures on collections were down when adjusted for population served and in constant dollars during these two recessions.

Not only did circulation increase, but the increases in interlibrary borrowing facilitated even greater access to materials requested during the two recessions. Perhaps this was partially necessitated by decreases in personal collection purchases. It also appears that remote access may have contributed to these requests that can be made remotely, but require visits to the libraries to pick up the materials. A June 2007 household telephone survey conducted for the ALA by Harris Interactive determined that the incidence of purchasing books, CDs, and DVDs after borrowing them from the library was significant. Forty-five percent of households surveyed reported purchasing a book (hardcover or softcover) after borrowing it from a library. Twenty-two percent of households reported purchasing CDs and DVDs after borrowing them from a library.[16]

Further evidence of circulation and the level of use of public library collections is given from the 2007 Library Survey in tables 9.20 and 9.21. Circulation was reported to be used extensively and with a substantial uptrend in use. The use of interlibrary borrowing in print and electronic format was much less than circulation, but to be expected because it is a substitute for the circulation of in-library materials that are not owned by the library, although the uptrend was substantial for both formats.

Total circulation of children's materials is compared with total circulation, and children's program attendance is given for the 1990s recession and the 2000s recession, respectively, in tables 9.22 and 9.23. Children's circulation was up in the 2000s recession, but not nearly as much as total circulation. Subtracting children's circulation from total circulation (i.e., 1,089 in 2000 and 1,293 in 2004) indicates an increase of 18.7 percent.

Table 9.20

Proportion (%) of Level of Use of Public Libraries, and Trend in Level Compared to Five Years Ago: 2007 (n = 431)

Service	LEVEL OF USE (%)			TREND IN USE (%)		
	Extensive	Often	Rare	Less	Same	More
Circulation	87.5	11.0	1.5	12.6	15.8	71.5
Current periodicals: Print	29.8	60.4	9.8	27.9	37.2	34.8
Print backfiles	79.3	18.4	2.3	8.6	37.9	53.5
E-book collection	3.6	45.7	50.8	53.9	31.5	14.6
E-journal collection	6.1	51.9	42.0	—	51.7	48.3
E-reports	19.7	55.4	24.8	3.4	27.7	68.9
Web portal to resources	41.8	47.2	10.8	1.9	13.0	85.1
Audiovisual collection	75.8	20.4	3.9	4.4	12.5	83.1

J. M. Griffiths and D. W. King, "A National Study of the Future of Public Librarians in the Workforce," 2009.

University of North Carolina at Chapel Hill, School of Information and Library Science, for the Institute of Museum and Library Services

Table 9.21

Proportion (%) of Interlibrary Borrowing Level of Use by Public Libraries, and Trend in Level Compared to Five Years Ago: 2007 (n = 431)

Service	LEVEL OF USE (%)			TREND IN USE (%)		
	Extensive	Often	Rare	Less	Same	More
Interlibrary borrowing: Print	36.1	51.3	12.6	13.8	26.0	60.2
Interlibrary borrowing: Electronic	16.7	47.9	35.4	12.5	27.1	60.4

J. M. Griffiths and D. W. King, "A National Study of the Future of Public Librarians in the Workforce," 2009.

University of North Carolina at Chapel Hill, School of Information and Library Science, for the Institute of Museum and Library Services

Reference transactions per capita have not changed much from 1990 to 2004, and the 2007 survey confirms this fact. The use of "general reference and research" is reported extensively in 29 percent of libraries, often in 54 percent, and rarely in 17 percent. The trend compared to five years ago is less in 28 percent of the libraries, about the same in 38 percent, and more in 34 percent, which balances with the less use.

One significant service provided by public libraries during the current recession (2009–2010) is support for job seeking. The ALA/Gates study identified seven such services:

▌ provides access to jobs databases and other job opportunity resources (88.2% of libraries)

▌ provides access to civil service exam materials (74.9%)

▌ offers software and other resources to help patrons create résumés and other employment materials (68.9%)

Table 9.22

Total Circulation in Public Libraries, Total Circulation of Children's Materials, and Children's Program Attendance during the Early 1990s Recession: 1990–1994

Year	Total Circulation (millions)	Circulation of Children's Materials (millions)	Children's Program Attendance (millions)
1990[1]	1,395	—	—
1991[1]	1,467	—	—
1992[1]	1,555	—	—
1993	1,586	462.9	35.6
1994	1,570	491.8	38.4
4-year change	+12.5%	+6.2%	+7.9%

1. These data began to be reported in 1993.

National Center for Education Statistics (now provided by Institute of Museum and Library Services), *Public Libraries in the United States.*

University of North Carolina at Chapel Hill, School of Information and Library Science, for the Institute of Museum and Library Services

Table 9.23

Total Circulation in Public Libraries, Total Circulation of Children's Materials, and Children's Program Attendance during the Early 2000s Recession: 2000–2004

Year	Circulation (millions)	Children's Materials (millions)	Children's Program Attendance (millions)
2000	1,714	624.7	49.3
2001	1,790	653.9	51.8
2002	1,898	682.9	52.1
2003	1,965	699.9	53.3
2004	2,001	708.3	54.6
4-year change	+16.7%	+13.4%	+10.8%

National Center for Education Statistics (now provided by Institute of Museum and Library Services), *Public Libraries in the United States.*

University of North Carolina at Chapel Hill, School of Information and Library Science, for the Institute of Museum and Library Services

▌ helps patrons complete online job applications (67.1%)

▌ offers classes (24.5%), collaborates with outside agencies or individuals to help complete job applications (23.6%), and develops business plans or other materials to start a business (14.2%).

Another important service provided during the current recession is access to government information and services: providing assistance in (1) accessing government websites (88.8% of libraries), (2) applying for or accessing government services (78.7%), (3) completing government forms (66.3%), (4) understanding government programs and services (43.3%), and (5) partnering with government agencies and others to provide services (20.5%), among many other helpful services. Public libraries have quickly adapted to provide services that are badly needed during a recession.

POSSIBLE COST-CUTTING MEASURES TAKEN BY PUBLIC LIBRARIES DURING TWO RECESSIONS

Both in-person and remote online visits to public libraries increased substantially during the two recessions, requiring additional staff (see chapter 6) as well as expenses. There are also some cost-cutting measures that apparently were taken. As mentioned above, expenditures for collections dampened during the two recessions when adjusted for population increases and in constant dollars. When the library collection is limited, public libraries increase borrowing materials from other libraries, and this activity has increased substantially as shown above. Even though there is an expense associated with each item borrowed, the borrowed item requires several uses (in the order of 10 to 20 uses, depending on the purchase price) to make it less expensive to purchase.

Another cost-cutting measure is to reduce the number of service hours. Evidence of this is provided by the NCES reporting the average number of weekly service hours per outlet by ranges of hours. Tables 9.24 and 9.25 display these estimates during the two recessions. The results show a decline in the proportion of public libraries with longer weekly hours during the recession.

Another way to examine the reduction in weekly hours is comparison of the actual number of public library outlets involved (table 9.26). This table shows a reduction in the number of libraries that were open over 60 hours during the recession. The libraries with outlets having few weekly hours (under 30) also decrease,

Table 9.24

Average Number of Public Library Weekly Public Service Hours per Outlet, by Ranges of Hours, during the Early 1990s Recession: 1990–1994

| Year | AVERAGE WEEKLY SERVICE HOURS (%) | | | | |
	0–29	30–49	50–59	60–69	70 or more
1990	40.2	37.5	13.7	7.3	1.2
1991	40.1	38.0	13.7	7.2	1.0
1992	38.9	39.6	13.7	7.0	0.8
1993	37.5	40.6	14.0	7.2	0.8
1994	36.8	40.7	14.4	7.3	0.8
4-year change	−8.5%	+8.5%	+5.1%	—	−33.3%

National Center for Education Statistics (now provided by Institute of Museum and Library Services), *Public Libraries in the United States.*

University of North Carolina at Chapel Hill, School of Information and Library Science, for the Institute of Museum and Library Services

Table 9.25

Average Number of Public Library Weekly Public Service Hours per Outlet, by Ranges of Hours, during the Early 2000s Recession: 2000–2004

| Year | AVERAGE WEEKLY SERVICE HOURS (%) | | | | |
	0–29	30–49	50–59	60–69	70 or more
2000	30.6	42.0	15.9	10.2	1.4
2001	29.7	42.3	16.3	10.4	1.2
2002	28.7	43.0	16.4	10.6	1.3
2003	28.0	43.3	17.3	10.2	1.2
2004	29.1	44.1	16.8	9.0	1.0
4-year change	−4.9%	+5.0%	+5.7%	−11.8%	−28.6%

National Center for Education Statistics (now provided by Institute of Museum and Library Services), *Public Libraries in the United States.*

University of North Carolina at Chapel Hill, School of Information and Library Science, for the Institute of Museum and Library Services

Table 9.26

Average Number of Public Library Weekly Public Service Hours per Outlet, by Ranges of Hours, during Two Recessions: 1990, 1994 and 2000, 2004

Range of Service Hours	NUMBER OF LIBRARIES			NUMBER OF LIBRARIES		
	1990	1994	Change	2000	2004	Change
0–9	503	366	−137	272	248	−24
10–19	1,293	1,169	−124	860	801	−59
20–29	1,814	1,749	−65	1,639	1,630	−9
30–39	1,742	1,873	+131	1,892	1,980	+88
40–49	1,625	1,757	+132	1,920	2,081	+161
50–59	1,230	1,285	+55	1,440	1,547	+107
60–69	655	651	−4	924	828	−96
70 or more	108	71	−37	127	92	−35
Total	8,970	8,921	−49	9,074	9,207	+133

National Center for Education Statistics (now provided by Institute of Museum and Library Services), *Public Libraries in the United States.*

University of North Carolina at Chapel Hill, School of Information and Library Science, for the Institute of Museum and Library Services

Table 9.27

Proportion (%) of Ranges of Hours per Week Open for One-on-One Responses in Public Libraries and Available In-Person and Internet/E-Mail Responses and Average Hours per Week: 2007

Type of Visit	Sample (n)	HOURS OPEN/AVAILABLE (%)				AVERAGE HOURS Open/Available
		<40	40 to 49	50 to 59	60 and over	
In-person	1,564	26.4	24.5	21.7	27.4	47.8
Internet/E-mail	1,548	29.6	22.7	18.5	29.2	49.2

J. M. Griffiths and D. W. King, "A National Study of the Future of Public Librarians in the Workforce," 2009.

University of North Carolina at Chapel Hill, School of Information and Library Science, for the Institute of Museum and Library Services

perhaps reflecting a reduction in bookmobiles and small branches. The tables also show that the number of libraries with over 60 hours increased substantially between recessions from 1994 to 2000 (i.e., from 722 libraries in 1994 to 1,051 in 2000), suggesting that the weekly hours increased in non-recession years.

The 2007 Library Survey provides further evidence of this (see table 9.27). This table indicates that 27.4 percent of public libraries were open 60 or more hours in 2007 compared with 10 percent in 2004.

EVIDENCE OF CHANGE BASED ON STATEWIDE SURVEYS DONE IN FLORIDA IN 2004 AND 2010

There were two statewide surveys done to determine the return on investment in Florida public libraries. The first, conducted in 2004 ("Taxpayer Return on Investment in Florida Public Libraries," by J. M. Griffiths, D. W. King, and others), involved household telephone interviews of 883 adults, in-library surveys of 1,505 adults (conducted with print questionnaires), and surveys of 138 other organizations. The second set of surveys, done in 2010 ("Taxpayer Return on Investment in Florida Public Libraries," 2010, by P. K. Pooley and others, Haas Center for Business Research and Economic Development, University of West Florida), involved household telephone interviews of 905 adults and a web-based survey of 2,094 adult library users. The 2010 surveys used the 2004 survey questions with few modifications and with some additional questions not discussed here. Both studies applied an econometric input-output model (REMI) covering 169 economic sectors for the state of Florida. This model established a long-term economic ripple effect of public libraries. Evidence of the impact of the current recession is given below for comparative demographics, visits, revenue, purpose of use, value, and return on investment.

There were some minor differences in the demographics of public library users. For example, in 2010 a higher proportion of females use the library, users tend to be more highly educated, and more are unemployed and looking for work or are not looking for work (10% in 2010 vs. 8% in 2004). A somewhat higher proportion of users are employed in government and more are retired. It is noted that in 2004 the country was just coming out of a recession while now it is in a deeper recession.

As observed elsewhere, public library visits increased during recessions. In 2004 there were 68.3 million visits (about 8 million by tourists), and in 2010 the total visits are estimated to be 94 million based on 2009 state statistics. The visits per capita were 4.0 in 2004 and increased to 5.0 in 2010. Based on the telephone surveys, the average number of in-person visits per visitor was 14.9 visits per visitor in 2004 and increased to 17.8 visits in 2010. The proportion of adults who said they connected to a public library remotely using the Internet in 2004 was 28.4 percent in 2004, increasing to 54.4 percent in 2010. However, perhaps due to the increase in the number of new remote visitors, the average visits per remote visitor decreased from 16.7 visits to 15.8 visits.

While visits increased, the libraries' revenue appears to be decreasing. Based on state statistics, the revenue decreased from $662 million in 2008 to $617 million in 2009 after increasing steadily since 2004. What is particularly relevant are the sources of revenue (table 9.28). Clearly, local funds assume an increased portion of the revenue. This has also been observed in the last two recessions.

The reasons users visit libraries are also changing to some extent. The proportion of visits for work-related purposes is up and that for educational purposes is down, while personal and recreational uses remain about the same. The proportion of work-related uses for starting a small business is down some, but visits for research, finance, and operations are up. The proportion of education-related uses by students is down while uses by teachers are up. Use for job hunting is up due to increased number of visits, but it is about the same for proportion of uses. Uses to learn about culture, religion, etc., are up the most among personal reasons for using the library. The average ratings of the importance of information provided by the library services in meeting needs is about the same for 2004 and 2010 users.

Table 9.28
Proportions (%) of Revenue Sources of Public
Libraries in Florida: 2004 and 2010

	PROPORTION (%) OF REVENUE SOURCES	
	2004	2010
Local	86.1	90.7
State	7.6	4.7
Federal	0.5	0.1
Other	5.8	4.5

J. M. Griffiths, D. W. King, et al., "Taxpayers Return on Investment in Florida Public Libraries," for the State Library and Archives of Florida, 2004.

P. K. Pooley, et al., "Taxpayer Return on Investment in Florida Public Libraries," Haas Center for Business Research and Economic Development, University of West Florida, 2010.

One indicator of the value of public libraries is the time users are willing to spend in the library on their visits. In 2004 the average time was 44 minutes per visit, but this increased to 55 minutes in 2010. Another indicator of value is contingent valuation, which is a method used to assess the benefits of non-priced goods and services by examining the implications of not having that product or service. This is determined by asking users what they would do if they didn't have a public library. Answers are: I would not bother to do anything (13% responded this way in 2004 and 10% in 2010); I need the information, but do not know where else to go (8% in 2004 and 16% in 2010); and I would use another source such as a store (79% in 2004 and 74% in 2010). The cost to use an alternative source was $4.05 billion in 2004 and $7.19 billion in 2010 (attributable in part to an increase in visits and inflation). A better indication is a net benefit in which library costs are subtracted from the cost of alternatives. These net costs were $2.33 billion and $4.29 billion in 2004 and 2010, respectively.

When all economic contributions are included in the return on investment in public libraries in Florida, there was an increase from 6.54 to 1 in 2004 to 8.32 to 1 in 2010. Part of this is due to a reduction in relative revenue because of the recession. A similar result is observed for the REMI analysis. For every dollar of public support spent on public libraries, the value of all goods and services produced (GRP) was $9.08 in 2004 and $15.57 in 2010. For every dollar of public support spent on public libraries, the income (wages) of Florida workers increased by $12.66 in 2004 and $22.97 in 2010. In 2004, for every $6,488 dollars of library support, one job was created in Florida, and this was much less at $3,491 in 2010. The economic return on investment has increased substantially from 2004 to 2010 even in light of the current recession.

Notes

1. American Library Association, "Libraries Connect Communities: Public Library Funding & Technology Access Study 2009–2010," 2010, available at www.ala.org/plinternetfunding. See also American Library Association, "A Perfect Storm Brewing: Budget Cuts Threaten Public

Library Services at a Time of Increased Demand," 2010, www.ala.org/ala/research/initiatives/plftas/issuesbriefs/issuebrief_perfectstorm.pdf.

2. The United States is currently in a deep recession. To gain some insight as to public-sector reaction to recessions, see Julie Hatch, "Employment in the Public Sector: Two Recessions' Impact on Jobs," *Monthly Labor Review* 127, no. 10 (October 2004), which sheds some light on the effect of past recessions (1990s and 2001) on employment in the public and private sectors. This is revealing because public libraries are part of the public sector. Portions of the article are quoted in appendix A of an IMLS-sponsored study (see the Web Extra supplement, available at www.alaeditions.org/webextras/). Some newspaper articles provide anecdotal evidence of the impact of the current recession (appendix B: see Web Extra). See J. M. Griffiths and D. W. King, "A National Study of the Future of Librarians in the Workforce," 2009, available at www.libraryworkforce.org.

3. M. D. Cooper, N. A. Van House, and N. K. Roderer, King Research, Inc., *Library Human Resources: A Study of Supply and Demand, 1983* (Chicago: American Library Association, 1983).

4. It is noted that the NCES data are estimates based on early reported data and may be underestimated due to a small proportion of non-responses that vary from year to year.

5. Griffiths and King, "A National Study."

6. D. M. Davis and T. D. Hall, "Diversity Counts," American Library Association, www.ala.org/ala/aboutala/offices/diversity/diversitycounts/diversitycounts_rev0.pdf.

7. Griffiths and King, "A National Study."

8. Institute of Museum and Library Services, "Public Libraries Survey: Fiscal Year 2007," 2009, http://harvester.census.gov/imls/pubs/pls/pub_detail.asp?id=122#.

9. U.S. Bureau of Labor Statistics, http://data.bls.gov/cgi-bin/print.pl/oco/ocos068.htm, in 2010–11 edition.

10. The total public libraries are single-outlet libraries that include a few bookmobiles. Stationary outlets exclude bookmobiles.

11. American Library Association, "A Perfect Storm Brewing."

12. Staff expenditures are largely fixed—tied to local government scales—and increase due to negotiated agreements (collective bargaining, etc.). As already noted, salaries and benefits can be as much as 70 percent of a library's operating budget and often cannot be reduced. The remaining 30 percent pays for everything else.

13. Griffiths and King, "A National Study."

14. NCES standards in early years note that variables with more than 30 percent missing data should not be used in analysis. Attendance in libraries exceeded this amount. If the non-responding libraries are typical, the amount would be 745 visits.

15. Griffiths and King, "A National Study."

16. Harris Interactive, "Purchasing Materials after Using a Public Library," www.ala.org/ala/research/librarystats/public/purchasing_after_use_omni_6_20.pdf.

   This study presents the results of three household surveys conducted during June 2007 to understand purchase-after-use patterns of youth (8–18 years) and adult (18 years and older) public library users.

Index

You may also be interested in

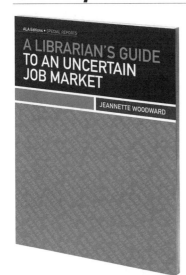

A LIBRARIAN'S GUIDE TO AN UNCERTAIN JOB MARKET

Jeannette Woodward

In this ALA Editions Special Report, Woodward helps at-risk librarians prepare for budget crunches, educate themselves about which library positions are being phased out and which will hold steady or expand, adjust their career goals, repurpose their existing skills for nontraditional librarianship, and even search for work in non-library settings.

ISBN: 978-0-8389-1105-1
112 PGS / 8.5" × 11"

CAREER DEVELOPMENT

WHAT THEY DON'T TEACH YOU IN LIBRARY SCHOOL
ELISABETH DOUCETT

ISBN: 978-0-8389-3592-7

WORKING IN THE VIRTUAL STACKS: THE NEW LIBRARY AND INFORMATION SCIENCE
EDITED BY
LAURA TOWNSEND KANE

ISBN: 978-0-8389-1103-7

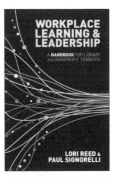

WORKPLACE LEARNING & LEADERSHIP: A HANDBOOK FOR LIBRARY AND NONPROFIT TRAINERS
LORI REED AND PAUL SIGNORELLI

ISBN: 978-0-8389-1082-5

ADMINISTRATION & MANAGEMENT

THE CHALLENGE OF LIBRARY MANAGEMENT: LEADING WITH EMOTIONAL ENGAGEMENT
WYOMA VANDUINKERKEN AND PIXEY ANNE MOSLEY

ISBN: 978-0-8389-1102-0

BE A GREAT BOSS
CATHERINE HAKALA-AUSPERK

ISBN: 978-0-8389-1068-9

DEALING WITH DIFFICULT PEOPLE IN THE LIBRARY, 2E
MARK R. WILLIS

ISBN: 978-0-8389-1114-3

Order today at **alastore.ala.org** or **866-746-7252!**

ALA Store purchases fund advocacy, awareness, and accreditation programs for library professionals worldwide.